ATTRACT HIM!

A Psychic Reveals How to Find Love and Romance

WILLIAM STILLMAN

First Edition:
First printing

PUBLISHED BY HAUNTED ROAD MEDIA, LLC
www.hauntedroadmedia.com

Cleveland, Ohio
United States of America

Other Books by William Stillman:

Autism and the God Connection

The Soul of Autism

The Autism Prophecies

Conversations with Dogs: A Psychic Reveals What Our Canine Companions Have to Say (And How You Can Talk to Them Too!)

Under Spiritual Siege: How Ghosts and Demons Affect Us and How to Combat Them

The Secret Language of Spirit: Understanding Spirit Communication in Our Everyday Lives

The Practicing Psychic: An Essential Guide for Staying Grounded, Navigating Skeptics, and Honoring Your Gift

TABLE OF CONTENTS

INTRODUCTION

As a practicing psychic medium since 2004, my clientele is about eighty-percent female, the age range of which is from roughly twenty years old to glorious gals in their eighties. All have been from very diverse backgrounds and cultures; some grew up in near-poverty and others have been quite well to-do. Some have never before been married and others have been married more than once. (I think the most married was a woman who had had seven husbands!) Some are also widowed, and sometimes widowed more than once (and, sadly, some have been widowed at a very young age). But, as you can imagine, each longs for companionship as would be expected and natural of most anyone.

In my history of working in the highly specialized field of giving intuitive advice, spiritual guidance, and communing with deceased loved ones, I can tell you without a doubt the single most frequently asked, impatiently presented question is: "When am I going to find a man?" Still others have pressed me for specifics such as, "What is his first name…his initials?" "Do I already know him?" "What will he look like?" "How will we meet?" and even, "Will we have children together, if so, how many?" At times it has felt a bit like an inquisition, so insistently have the questions been posed.

As you might also imagine, there is no one pat response to such probing inquiries simply because it is such an individualized process and, importantly, because love is not a one-size-fits-all prospect. But there have been enough commonalties to draw some conclusions about this business of finding and keeping a man and achieving true love. Those commonalities have been culled from the intuitive impressions I have received in my one-on-one interactions with my clients. Most amazing of all, I have additionally been enlightened and informed directly by my clients' loved ones who are communicating through me from the Other Side. All of which has culminated in the book you now hold in your hands.

I have always viewed my objective as a psychic medium to be that of working myself out of a job. I have also always had as my policy a once-annual, one-hour session. And that has been firm. The reason for this is twofold. First, some of what is discussed, and even predicted, requires time to percolate and simmer before manifesting. That could take three, six, nine months or more; but ultimately, and more often than not, it all does, indeed, come to fruition. Second, I have never wanted to foster a dependency on my services. Believe me, I have had people cry, beg and plead; and attempt to coax, cajole and bribe me to do differently—but I refuse to budge. I could easily have the same clients rotating through on a bi-weekly basis but that would be terribly unhealthy, in my opinion. And to do business otherwise only fuels the stereotype that all psychics are scam artists, grifters and financial vampires.

The fundamental truths disclosed in each individual session, and which are offered here as well, are not rocket science or so profound as to be out of reach of the average human being. They are, in fact, very, very simple—and there's a great beauty in that sentiment. Everything I'm sharing with you here is obtainable, but you have to want it! And oftentimes "wanting it" requires that we go within to examine our motives, reflect upon our history, and come to terms with ourselves. However, I am confident that this experience, if pursued with due diligence, will bear fruit.

My hope is that Attract Him! will serve as a resource to those who have tired of online dating; dread mismatched or blind dates; and have, seemingly, exhausted other alternatives to the point of giving up hope. This book is not for those who enjoy casual encounters, fun flirtations or forbidden affairs. But if you are serious in finding a man who is long-term or marriage material, this book may prove invaluable. Strangely enough, the easiest route is the spiritual route although it is most often overlooked. It's an option that has been there all along, but it may have been suppressed or dormant. This book is designed to get you back on a romantic track. Perhaps most significantly, it is designed to empower you with a greater understanding of yourself and just how much of your own journey is truly self-directed.

Chapter 1

BREAKING OLD PATTERNS

You are a product of your environment and upbringing. If your upbringing was generally pleasant and your family was loving and supportive for the most part, suffice it to say you are, yourself, probably well-adjusted. It is advantageous to have been raised by parents who disciplined in ways that were fair and reasonable; who regularly praised and encouraged; and who had great expectations for your promising future. This manifests in a confidence and self-esteem that comes of knowing you've got family who are your greatest champions and your most ardent cheerleaders.

I have to say, however, that this scenario tends to be the exception to the rule in my work anymore. I know that some people feel great shame and guilt because their family background includes mental and physical abuse, infidelity, illegitimate children, alcoholism or even incest, but let me tell you, it's all a lot more commonplace that you might think. Of course, these things weren't openly discussed decades ago and were termed "family secrets" for being so taboo and socially disgraceful. The family dysfunction becomes normalized such that it strongly influences one's ideas about relationships. These thought patterns are often genetically coded into one's DNA by virtue of one's heredity. In short, you may be naturally predisposed to having depression or being dependent or addicted because of your family history—and that's not your fault. (If you are adopted or otherwise unaware of your biological lineage, you can make respectful best guesses based upon your own self-evaluation and the vulnerabilities you can identify within yourself that have consistently surfaced over time.)

What I find so fascinating, from both a psychological and a spiritual perspective, is that the people who come from sordid pasts must face a challenge: To surrender to it or to overcome it. Surrendering to it is akin to the old adage, "If you can't beat 'em, join 'em." That is, if someone's father was a serial cheater who was often absentee and their mother was a depressed alcoholic, there is a vulnerability to be tempted to "play the victim card." What this means is that because someone has survived a tragic past—be it foster home placements or psychological abuse or sexual molestation—they feel it permissible to project an attitude of entitlement. They may adopt a position of arrogance, of emotional reserve, or of bias and prejudice. They may be unkind and insensitive in judging and critiquing others. Bitterness, despair and cynicism is apparent in most interactions. They may feel owed and obligated to have "only the best" of everything because of all they endured. This is not only a smokescreen to obscure the truth, it is a denial of truth. And it is merely an explanation, not an excuse.

People who project an attitude of entitlement tend to do so because they are protecting a façade which, oftentimes, has been very carefully constructed over many years. The façade is to shutter away the truth, in the way of suppressing family secrets. It is also intended to exert control by holding others at emotional arm's length. These people are struggling with old thought patterns of poor self-esteem, weak self-image, and self-loathing. But instead of trying to repair the damage, they reflect back what has been projected upon them by others. I know, because I was once one of them. It is easy to see, then, how a vicious and never-ending cycle ensues in which happiness and true love become elusive.

Suffice it to say, when you consistently emit low-energy, low-frequency vibrations, you will have a tremendous tendency to attract to you low-energy, low-frequency vibrations. This is because of the weak and muted "signal" you project. Like attracts like. This is fundamental physics and extends to relationships with neighbors, co-workers, family, and, of course, romantic relationships. I have seen time and again how effortlessly some women attract to them men who are versions of their own father, someone who was flawed and impaired and struggled with addictions. It is oftentimes all they expect; or they believe they can reverse the misconduct (more about this in Chapter Five).

Ever know someone for whom everything always seems to go wrong? I do. I know someone who always seems angry, anxious and in a state of annoyed agitation. Every other sentence that issues from this person's mouth is a complaint. And nine times out of ten, everything this person touches totally malfunctions. I have grown accustomed to this person whining about their phone not working, the computer freezing up, or appliances fritzing out. This happens with such regularity and yet this person isn't able to (or is unwilling to) connect the dots and trace the origins of it all back to themselves.

Amazingly, some people stuck in this modality portend to be the very opposite by temporarily aligning themselves with a healthy lifestyle. While this shows an effort to move in the right direction, they, themselves, do not look like the healthy product or program they are promoting. They turn on a different façade that feigns positivity but only for so long as it is needed. How can someone inspire others to engage in a healthy lifestyle if they, themselves, drink and smoke, overeat, and spew curses cynically when off guard? This is duplicitous. If you are not conducting yourself consistently and with transparency across all environments, you cannot be considered authentic.

Additionally, the longer someone remains caught in this inauthentic pattern of thought, the more likely they are to become physically ill. This occurs when the negative thinking and misconduct transfers from the mental-emotional domain to the physical domain. This, in turn, manifests in fatigue and loss of energy, as well as physical ailments that compromise the body's immune system. It is a tremendous stress to constantly endure dark and heavy thoughts. Believe it or not, I have seen people who are not nice and who behave badly work themselves into cancer. It is inevitable when one's thoughts are almost exclusively comprised of hate, jealousy, bitterness, prejudice, and so on. Linger long enough in the muck and mire of the lowest-vibration human emotions and it cannot help but to erode you on all levels and across your three domains. By this, I am referring to your mental-emotional, physical, and spiritual well-being. More about these domains will be explained in the discussion on evolving in Chapter Three.

In contrast to the preceding, I can nearly always single out the person who has overcome the obstacles of their past. The tend to be the folks who have a positive glow about them. They seem to radiate goodness, hope and optimism. They are the proverbial person who "lights up a room" when they walk into it. There is literally a luminescence about them because they have instigated a transformation from the inside out. In so doing, they have not only improved the quality of their life, they have extended their life expectancy. I know a woman in her late nineties who is a perfect example of this. She always seems cheerful, looks on the bright side of any situation, and always has a kind word to say. But according to her doctors, she shouldn't be here. You see, she was diagnosed with pancreatic cancer. Because of her age—and because she experiences no pain or discomfort—her family has chosen not to reveal this to her. If ignorance is bliss, she has bliss in spades. To date, she has outlived the medical community's predictions of her demise by over three years. And that is a fine example of the power of positive thought.

The human mind is such a powerful tool. It sounds like a tired cliché to say so, but the key to breaking old patterns is to illuminate the truth in your own consciousness. Your past can no longer plague you if you call it out by identifying the sources, or triggers, that contribute to the perpetual cycle. The bottom line, in its simplest form, is that you are not a victim. The victim routine is the easy way out and will eventually fall on deaf ears, as those who are drained by the constant drama will retreat and withdraw. You were placed in challenging circumstances and presented with struggles for a reason—a spiritual purpose or, if you prefer, an ethereal throw-down.

Try to think about your life history from an objective point of view, as another person might see it or as if you were sitting on the moon looking down at this ridiculous soap opera that plays out down here. If you can assume this perspective, you may be better poised to take responsibility for the things you have done and said that were hurtful, even harmful, to others. If you don't do it while you're here, you'll eventually have to do it in Heaven. It is not unheard of for a client's deceased mother or father to come through in one of my private sessions to express their regret for having only learned difficult lessons once they got to where they are now. It's called a life review.

No one is forced or coerced into a life review, but it is understood that, in order for a soul to advance, it is necessary. Oftentimes, I am shown that it is very much like being seated alone in a movie theater. On screen, various scenes from our life are projected. It is an opportunity for self-critique, to acknowledge the good things but to also take responsibility for our bad acts and misdeeds. Usually, there is the sensation of experiencing the worst of what we've dished out from the emotional perspective of those on the receiving end. The purpose for this is twofold; it is intended to be a humbling experience but the knowledge and understanding gained is then imprinted within the composition of one's soul. The idea is that the soul will evolve in ways that reflect these improvements. But, you can get out ahead of this process while you are still here in human form! This is when it will have the greatest, most significant impact—and you'll score major spiritual "points" for figuring it out while you are still here.

This concept contributes to the idea that you are now engaged in the act of becoming, instead of remaining stuck and stagnant, as you had been. Now you may feel as though you are gaining momentum. If you can admit that you have some work to do in terms of personal "housecleaning," congratulations! That's a step beyond the person in denial who points the finger of blame at everyone except themselves. One of the great obstacles to breaking old patterns is a variety of fears. Don't permit fear to rule you. What kind of fear? Fear of losing your identity. Fear of losing friends. Fear of getting old. Fear of being lonely and abandoned. Fear of not being good enough, smart enough, pretty enough. Fear of being unloved.

When one is depressed and anxious, these are the types of thoughts that tend to loop repeatedly in our head. These negative internal dialogues are designed to berate and belittle us. They intend to wear us down, to provoke us into procrastination or to relapse such that breaking old patterns seems insurmountable. But are these thoughts really your own? When you hear these thoughts, is it even in your own voice or is it a different voice? Who is in control here? This residue from a dysfunctional upbringing and a history of bad relationships can take on a life of its own, and that is destructive to your upward mobility. Here are a series of exercises to consider as you become more conscious and aware.

Exercise #1: Whenever you feel your own thoughts being interrupted and intruded upon by negative thinking, stop whatever you are doing in the moment. Confront the thoughts that are hindering your ability to become an improved version of your old self. In a firm, authoritative voice, say out loud, "This is not helpful. This is not kind or loving. This is unwanted. I banish and expel all such thoughts that do not serve my greater good right here and now!" Or, try the shorthand version with a simple and direct, "I know what you're trying to do, now knock it off!" Develop a good habit of employing this technique as often as is necessary and you should see your need for its use diminish over time.

Exercise #2: Initiate the life review process by relieving yourself of burdens for carrying negative emotions tied to past events or people. This is a process that will take time. Do not attempt to do all of this in one sitting. Get yourself in a quiet space and try to identify the source or sources of the personality traits you'd like to improve or shed. It may be unpleasant to dredge up old memories, but this should be a healing opportunity to forgive and release. Consider how these sources have influenced how you treat yourself and others. For every uncomfortable or unpleasant memory you recall, and for which you take personal responsibility, counter it by recalling a memory in which you were kind and helpful. This will lend balance to the process and should dissuade you from feeling overwhelmed or defeated.

Exercise #3: Spend some time dissecting what you inhale, what you eat, and what you drink. Is there room for improvement? Are there things that you have historically used as crutches? Things that are not healthy for us often smell and taste really good. Indulging in something unhealthy can also make us feel good, but only temporarily. After the sensation wears off, we usually feel worse for having overindulged. People who smoke know that it's bad for them. People who drink too much know it's not healthy. People who overeat and eat unhealthy foods know it's a vicious cycle too. But you can't eat what you don't buy, and if it's not in the house, it's not there to consume. Are there things you can be doing to create a shift, to minimize what you ingest, and to better reflect trends toward improved health? Again, this is not a cold-turkey process but one that should occur gradually and with determined effort.

Exercise #4: How much of your time is consumed with text-messaging, emailing, and posting and responding on social media? Ever notice that people do and say things online they probably wouldn't in person, face-to-face? This kind of unpleasantness has caused some social platforms and news outlets to discontinue permitting comments to be posted. Friendships and relationships have been terminated as a result of miscommunications or insensitive communications posted to social media. Have you found yourself tempted to join the fray of heated debates? Have you felt compelled to choose sides between friends? Or have you distanced yourself from friends or even family members because of their online conduct. As you know, things can become toxic very quickly, none of which contributes to evolving the energy you emit. Consider how to limit and curtail your time in favor of powering down and doing something creative and productive.

Exercise #5: Be conscious of reversing not just your own negative thoughts but those of others. Remember, if you have been stuck in this mode of thought, there's a high probability that you have others around who think and behave similarly. Sometimes this is simply inescapable because those who are prejudiced or pessimistic may actually live under the same roof with you. Try a little experiment: For every negative comment you hear someone make, counter it by saying something positive or complimentary. For example, if you're watching television and someone says something derogatory about someone's appearance, you can respond by saying, "She's got beautiful skin and great eyes!" At first, it may not register but you may just be delighted to see how, slowly but surely, those who are accustomed to making nasty comments and snide remarks begin to follow suit. In this manner, you are leading by example and invisibly so.

These exercises are a solid foundation for the process of dismantling harmful cycles and breaking old patterns of thought. Again, this is all a process not to be rushed but to be implemented gradually and with deliberation. None of this is intended to be discouraging; please don't avoid doing it because you think it will be too painful a process. Remember, the intention is to evolve yourself into an improved version of your old self, so that you radiate positive, healthy energy and are poised to attract similar energy to you in return. No one is obligated to remain stuck in old patterns because that is how people have always known and identified you. Your transformation is imminent, but you have to want it; and only you, alone, can initiate it.

William Stillman

Chapter 2

A BAD RELATIONSHIP ISN'T ALWAYS A BAD THING

In the last chapter, it was discussed how some women have a great tendency to attract to them men who are struggling and wounded, who oftentimes share in common many of the same dysfunctional traits of each woman's own father. It is a bittersweet cycle that plays out across any number of malfunctioning relationships that these women have convinced themselves they can save. Desperation and urgency to have a man, to be in a relationship at all costs, and to be wanted can actually create blockages to emitting and receiving healthy and positive energy—the very kind that will generate strong connections and will endure over time. But not every relationship is intended to be happily ever after. Furthermore, allow me to preface this chapter by stating clearly that no one should permit themselves to be in a relationship in which they are mentally-emotionally, physically, or sexually abused. Having said that, there are certainly valuable lessons to be learned from surviving an unhappy or abusive relationship.

In my psychic work, it has been so fascinating to be privy to a unique phenomenon that has occurred since the dawn of time but seems to have been most commonplace in the 1930s and throughout the World War II era: the preponderance of love at first sight. I cannot tell you the number of times I have channeled someone's deceased parent or grandparent who will relay to me that when they first laid eyes on their future mate, they said aloud, "That's the girl I'm going to marry," or "That boy doesn't know it yet but he's going to marry me." What's so intriguing is that these circumstances seem to have occurred quite randomly and by happenstance—something we'll revisit in Chapter Twelve. It's almost as if some divine force was at play (and maybe, in fact, that's precisely what it was) to foster loving bonds in a generation of people who needed to unite and sustain during very trying times.

These couples rarely divorced and were committed to one another until they were separated by death. They created their futures, their families, and their lives together with such intention and determination, sheer "grit" if you will. Curiously, this commitment to one another is exactly what so often buoyed those relationships through the proliferation of men who returned home from having served in overseas combat suffering with what we now know was post-traumatic stress disorder, or "shell shock," as it was known then. The sense of loyalty, devotion and, yes, duty between wives and their husbands aided them to persevere as well as could be.

Frequently, these men became alcoholics in order to suppress their nightmares and cope with their re-entry back into society after having had to endure truly horrific experiences that no human being should. I have been shown countless times in psychic sessions that, in combat, these men lost friends and good buddies who had their heads, arms and legs blown off in front of them. Precisely this was confirmed in a recent psychic reading in which my client's deceased World War II veteran grandfather came through to apologize for being so quiet and reserved. He showed me that he was witness to army friends being killed before his very eyes and, indeed, my client confirmed that it was her grandfather's mission to locate and navigate mine fields.

These men struggled with anger and rage or became very emotionally guarded and withdrawn as a result. They came home broken, and very different from how they left. It was stigmatizing to seek psychiatric support at that time; instead, they were told to forget about what happened, that it was in the past, and to get on with their lives, as if it could simply be turned on and off like a light switch. The client in the preceding paragraph's example told me that her grandmother once shared with her what had happened to her grandfather and discouraged her from ever asking her grandfather about his military service as he, understandably, didn't wish to discuss it.

These World War II veterans, and to a lesser extent veterans of the Korean War and Vietnam, were the fathers, grandfathers, and great-grandfathers of many men who are with us today. In the last chapter, the potential for the genetic and environmental vulnerabilities of our upbringing was shown to affect our thought patterns, behavior, and who and what we attract to us. The same is true of the sons, grandsons and great-grandsons of these very men; they, too, have tremendous potential to experience all of the same mental-emotional health issues. And as you may know, many of these families are military families, meaning that there is a long history of men and women serving in military service.

The "love at first sight" phenomenon of the 1930s and '40s seems to have dissipated significantly in more recent times; it doesn't seem nearly as widespread as it had been at one time. Things appear to have shifted given how advances in technology have affected how people connect, such as through online dating sites. What has also shifted since the 1930s and '40s is the de-stigmatization of divorce and the acceptability of couples living together prior to marriage. And so, social mores and expectations are much looser and freer than decades earlier when people felt an obligation and social expectation to remain married. This doesn't mean that the relationship problems are any less complex than they had been, they're just out in the open.

Not only are large numbers of men living today a reflection of their genetic heritage, your own father or grandfathers could also have been similarly affected. If you grew up in a dysfunctional household, then perhaps you, too, were exposed to a father or stepfather who was alcoholic, mentally cruel, physically abusive or sexually promiscuous. Once during a guided meditation, a member of a class I was teaching became overwrought with emotion. Tears streaming down her face, she explained that she couldn't stay and must leave immediately.

During the meditation, she had spontaneously re-experienced a long-suppressed memory of her father's sexual molestation of her, and she was overcome by the unexpected feelings the memory conjured. She needed some fresh air and time to process what had just occurred.

Growing up in a household with an emotionally detached or abusive father has the potential to create a false equivalency in the mind of someone already lacking in confidence and self-esteem. Being unable to see the forest for standing smack-dab in the middle of the trees may predispose one to believing that all fathers behave this way and, by extension, many men. Thus, there is great potential for women who were raised in such an environment to attract to them someone who is similar to their own father. The loss of fatherly love and acceptance may be experienced, by association, through the boyfriend, lover or husband during the "honeymoon" phase of the romantic relationship.

The fulfillment received during this timeframe may feel positively euphoric, almost a vindication. There is also often a sense of accompanying guilt for feeling undeserving of such happiness. But if the male in the relationship is also from a dysfunctional upbringing (as is the case when like attracts like), then the romance of the courtship is short lived before his true colors begin revealing themselves. I have known countless women who married very young to escape an abusive home life and wed first husbands who turned out to be virtual carbon copies of their own fathers. But because they didn't know any better, they didn't expect any better. This culture is still very much prevalent in this day and age.

29

Women who have found themselves in this situation are often pregnant before, or shortly after, marriage; and so, the situation becomes compounded with the introduction of a baby or more than one child. Taken for granted as normal are the flaws, faults and frailties of a husband who is unable to reciprocate loving emotions for growing up in an abusive household himself. Time and again I have been shown in private sessions, with my female clients, how confusing it is for their current, or former, husbands and boyfriends, to have such conflicted feelings for their own fathers. And consistently, when I am able to channel those deceased fathers, they share their remorse for causing their sons to doubt their loyalty and question if their own father even really much cared for them. It gives bittersweet credence to the adage "too little, too late."

In the manner that detached and depressed women may be overly critical, cynical and judgmental as mothers, men who emit low emotional energy tend to manifest it by becoming narcissists. Again, this is usually in keeping with the trajectory of family history. Their fathers, who were filled with self-loathing themselves, may have had unrealistically high expectations and impossible standards. Compliments, if ever given, would often be conditional such as saying, "You played a pretty good game, but your pitch could stand improvement." Narcissists have an overinflated opinion of their own self-worth. They are often liars, manipulators and braggarts focused only on fulfilling their own needs and bolstering their ego. They can also be very controlling and dominant, and this extends to sexual activities designed to humiliate and degrade in order to maintain and control their wife's or girlfriend's submission.

Oftentimes, when I am channeling a deceased ex-husband or father who behaved in this manner, they show me a visual fluctuation between Dr. Jekyll and Mr. Hyde, of the famous Robert Louis Stevenson gothic novel. In other words, they vacillated from one personality to another; the big, gregarious, outgoing public personality and the vicious, abusive and spiteful private personality. The irony of the narcissist is that they actually have very weak self-image and very low self-esteem. The brash-talking, self-complimenting Jekyll-and-Hyde persona is a façade, a safety net and a coping mechanism. Once these types reach the Heavenly realm, they tend to show me how they had erected a wrought-iron fence around their heart, secured with many padlocks so that no one can get in. (Of course, that has all been dismantled once in Heaven.)

Relationships such as these become a perfect storm, unless and until the male has an awakening and exerts time and effort into transforming. When this happens, it is usually due to a motivating factor, tragic event, or ultimatum. Once he determines to act upon his commitment, these men seek counseling and therapy, such as anger management; and they put forth effort into extinguishing dependencies and addictions. For never having had positive role models, so many of these men don't know how to be effective fathers or to even love their own spouse and children. It doesn't come easily or naturally for them so it must be learned because they don't even love themselves.

Regrettably, in my experience the men who can overcome have been the exception to the rule; and most often the marriage ends in divorce. Out of necessity, and even for fear of their safety and that of their children, women somehow find the courage to realize that their husband will never change. They have exhausted their patience and abandoned the fairy tale ending. Interestingly enough, during my psychic sessions with such women, oftentimes a grandmother or great grandmother will come through to support their decision. They will often suggest, "Do you think I had a happy marriage?" going on to state that females of modern times have many more options and resources available to them. In a long-ago era, divorce was simply not an option for the social disgrace it brought, especially in very religious families.

Once the break has been made, maintaining distance with the abusive partner is oftentimes easier said than done, particularly if there are children involved. Some of these men will threaten violence or will repeatedly threaten to harm themselves, which creates great worry, concern and anxiety if the former spouse has visiting privileges with the children. There have been several instances in which I've been shown in a psychic reading that the former husband or boyfriend has a gun or guns in his home. I then hear a gunshot ring out loud and clear—not as a harbinger of tragedy but as a warning to be especially cautious of the potential for what the future may hold. It is sometimes unclear if the gunshot is self-inflicted or if it is an indicator to avoid escalating confrontations with this person for fear of him making the worst-possible impulsive decision.

If you have endured terminating an unhealthy and abusive relationship, you are truly a survivor if you have risen beyond the circumstances to achieve a new level of understanding. This is authentic evolution. If you are indeed this person, then you possess the ability to compartmentalize the past in proper context and within the grand scheme of the big picture. It takes grace and courage to truly appreciate that a bad relationship isn't always a bad thing once you have correctly interpreted the experience as a learning opportunity and not a punishment. People who extract themselves from toxic relationships oftentimes do so by sheer will of determination. They seek support from formal and informal resources such as community agencies and family and friends. And they strive for self-improvement in the manner of furthering their education or training in order to become more self-reliant and less dependent.

The growth that transpires grants credence to the adage that from adversity grows success. Many successful, financially independent women have struggled through very challenging pasts to attain their success. Such a goal is not only a personal benchmark of achievement, it's a spiritual hallmark as well. In time, the wise woman is able to reconcile with gratitude her harrowing experiences because she realizes it all contributed to the journey of who she has become today. And that ain't a bad thing.

– Chapter 3 –

EVOLVING

The previous chapter concluded by examining how surviving a bad relationship may actually be the impetus that fuels an evolution of personal growth and spiritual strength. But, more specifically, what does that entail? The concept of evolving starts with being conscious and aware. You might be thinking, "But I am already conscious and aware! I'm conscious and aware of what I'm doing, where I'm going, and with whom I need to interact in order to get through my day!" That's all true, but that is being conscious and aware on a different level than the consciousness and awareness that permits one to engage in the act of becoming. Becoming is the serenity and confidence of knowing that you are entitled to your place in the Universe as well as the space that you occupy because you were placed here with deliberate intention. Becoming is dynamic, not static, because you are perpetually evolving and becoming an improved version of your old self. Becoming grants one permission to appreciate that there are no coincidences or accidents, that everything happens for a reason.

How does one reach that pinnacle of comprehension? I suggest a pathway that I have devised, and which has proven fruitful for others, that addresses three fundamental domains of our personhood: mental-emotional, physical and spiritual well-being. Being conscious and aware of these domains on a daily basis will not only facilitate your becoming, but it will also uplift your consciousness and your awareness so that you will be poised to attract a man that is a similar, high-caliber quality human being.

Achieving balance of the first domain, mental-emotional well-being, may be easier said than done depending upon your genetic history, childhood upbringing, past romantic relationships, and day-to-day obligations and responsibilities. The potential for your genetic history to affect this domain in ways that are a detriment have already been discussed but the piece of awareness that may be new is placing your heredity in the context of how it influences you in the here and now. A careful review of the addictions, dependencies and mental health issues, known or rumored, in paternal and maternal lineage could very well answer a lot of outstanding questions about your own conduct and perhaps that of your siblings.

If this vulnerability affected your childhood upbringing, have you invested time and effort into working through the ways in which you may have been affected, such as by depression, anxiety, post-traumatic stress disorder, and poor self-image and low self-esteem? I'd venture to suggest that the answer is "yes" if you have come this far, have survived the worst of your past and you are reading this book. Oftentimes, the abused becomes the abuser for reflecting back what has been projected upon him or her. If this has been true of yourself, in what ways have you portrayed yourself as a victim? People who are in victim mode are not only bitter and cynical, they are rarely satisfied because nothing seems to please them. They frequently curse using foul language angrily. An entitlement attitude may also be apparent for believing the very best is due them for all they endured. But in actuality, this is a stagnant and toxic position in which to operate.

It is okay to confess that you have behaved in victim mode previously. The acknowledgment itself is a sign of maturity and positive growth. Just as you wouldn't wish to go back to living in a toxic relationship, nor would you wish to revert back to your former way of being if you were bitter and cynical. But in both instances, there's a learning opportunity if you are able to change course, shift direction and self-determine a new pathway for yourself. This process requires a self-assessment and a life review (as was previously suggested as an exercise in Chapter One) in which you may reflect upon the good, the bad and the ugly in your personal history. Once you determine to think differently about how you treat yourself and others, you will disrupt old patterns and create new and healthy ones. The concept is not much different from Cognitive Behavior Therapy used by psychiatrists and other mental health clinicians; essentially replacing derailing and negative thoughts with proactive ones.

The second domain is physical health and well-being. An

exercise in Chapter One suggested contemplation for ways to address your body's welfare. When you think about it, our bodies are truly miraculous machines when they operate properly. Everything functions in harmony and with such intelligent design. Food goes in one end and, after its nutrients have been extrapolated, waste comes out the other end. Some body parts serve more than one function, and everything works in such unison that it is very easy to take it all for granted. We can even reproduce. Nothing ever needs to be plugged in or recharged—or does it?

When we fail our bodies, by not eating properly or getting enough sleep and exercise, we fail ourselves. Our body can only coast on fumes for so long before it starts to sputter out and fall apart. You've witnessed this yourself in people who ate and drank and smoked and otherwise ingested whatever they wanted their entire lives with a devil-may-care attitude. It eventually catches up with them, sometimes very early in life. They may become dependent on pharmaceuticals, oxygen, physical therapies, or support to eat, speak and ambulate reliably. You may have also noticed that such people age quite rapidly for treating their physical form so carelessly; they prematurely appear much older than their chronological years.

Conversely, people who are mindful of being kind and gracious and polite seem ageless. I have a friend who recently turned 105 years old. She was one of only thirteen people who survived a plane crash in the late 1940s. One of her feet was badly mangled and she was told she would never dance again, which was particularly devastating as she was a professional dancer. But with daily prayer and a renewed faith for having been spared her life from the tragedy, her foot healed. Not only that, she danced again. Given a new lease on life, my friend embraced her spirituality and became a student of metaphysics, learning all she could about being conscious and aware in human form. And best of all, she glows with youthful radiance and her eyes twinkle with warmth and wisdom. We should all be so fortunate.

Tending to your physical well-being isn't about plastic surgery or any other elective (and invasive) procedure in order to transform yourself. If it will aid you in feeling more attractive, do it but do it for yourself and not to please someone else. Besides, the average man doesn't pay attention to details in the manner that many women agonize over their perceived flaws. Men are "big picture" creatures who take in the totality of the entire person. They tend to overlook lumps, bumps, moles, cellulite, a few extra pounds or other things you may consider embarrassing imperfections.

Just as the human body is a self-contained and independently functioning organism, our planet provides for all of our nutritional needs. There has been an increasing trend among many people to shift toward a plant-based diet. If you choose to do so, first consult with your physician and a dietician to craft a regimen tailored to your personal needs. I'm not telling you what to eat but if you choose to consume the flesh of living creatures, please know that you are also consuming the trauma of the slaughter that is imprinted throughout that animal's physiology on a cellular level. The choice is entirely yours, but you may wish to limit how often you eat meat for this reason. You are also likely to feel physically "lighter" for tapering the amount meat you consume.

You will recall that your family history impacts your tendencies for dependencies. Many women are emotional eaters, meaning they use food, oftentimes unhealthy food, to contain or squelch altogether their emotions. High blood sugar and diabetes can also be inherited. Consider how often you, yourself, may reach for something sweet to treat or placate yourself for being stressed. If you smoke nicotine or marijuana, drink alcohol regularly, or use prescription medication for pain management or to treat a mental health issue, know that you are routinely altering the delicate balance of your body chemistry. If this pertains to you, perhaps addressing your physical health and well-being involves exploring options to lessen dependency in favor of holistic alternatives such as natural, herbal supplements, meditation and exercise. In recent times, drug stores and grocery stores have sections devoted to vitamins and supplements to consider as additions to, or instead of, pharmaceuticals. Remember, however, this is a process and one that should be deliberate yet gradual.

The third domain, you'll recall, is that of spiritual well-being. When I was young, I struggled with a spiritual assault that was so insidious that I only realized its effects in hindsight. I was bullied and harassed on an almost daily basis but had no one to tell and no support system of any kind, including spiritual. Unfortunately, I became filled with self-loathing and depression and became attracted to dark and unhealthy things. This skewed my perspective on people, causing me to become distrusting and cynical. It also hindered my ability to love. At that time, my understanding of God was limited, compartmentalized to ninety minutes on occasional Sunday mornings; I didn't expand the concept of God to include personal and immediate accessibility at any given moment. If I had, I might have powered through a very challenging time feeling successful and confident.

When I teach my intuition classes I often tell my students, God is not Santa Claus. In other words, God is not a friend with benefits if you only focus on the benefits you stand to gain from the friendship. Think of it this way: You wouldn't contact someone with whom you have had no communication since high school and ask to borrow a thousand dollars. It would be socially inappropriate and extremely awkward. The same may be said of a relationship with God. (As a side note, I use the word "God" because it is the word with which I was raised and with which I am most comfortable; however, it doesn't matter to me if you call it Source, Higher Power, Universe, Wonder Woman—whatever works for you, so long as you are owing reverence to, and honoring, the source of our creation.)

If your spiritual well-being is lacking and could use a tune-up, consider connecting to God for a few minutes on a daily basis. No, I'm not talking about a church or temple or other physical place of worship; nor am I discouraging that. But this is about connecting to the place in your heart and not necessarily a brick-and-mortar locale. This communication can occur in prayer or in a meditation. Either way, when you do so, you are practicing use of one of your spiritual gifts—telepathy!

Telepathy is the ability to silently send thoughts, dreams, wishes, hopes and desires to another with the expectation that they will be received, heard and acted upon. It may make sense to pray at times of transitioning between activities, while out walking or driving (eyes on the road though!), or while otherwise engaged in a meaningful activity. For example, if you are preparing a meal for family or friends, pause to express gratitude for having these people in your life.

I would not recommend that you pray for a man out of urgency or desperation. That will only create an internal conflict for you should you begin to doubt your faith if your prayers are not answered with the immediacy you expect. Instead, pray with deep gratitude and grateful appreciation for all that you are already so blessed to have received. In essence, begin by counting your blessings, essentially taking stock of all the many ways in which you have been saved and rescued, blessed and privileged over the course of your lifetime. Doing this regularly will not only elevate your spiritual consciousness, but it will also elevate the quality of energetic vibrations you are emitting so that you can attract a similar energy to you. Of course that's not why you do it, because you want a man; do it because it is the proper response to honoring your humanity.

Being aware of your mental-emotional, physical and spiritual well-being on a daily basis has the potential to manifest in greater opportunities for you to "do what you are." What this means is that you will find your thinking becomes more creative and inspired. You may revisit and reclaim dormant interests you had in childhood or adolescence, rediscovering with childish wonder what captivated you in your youth. You may also feel called to explore new things and to learn a new skill. This might look like signing up for an art class, a cooking class or taking a yoga or Pilates class. You might also register for other educational opportunities. You may find yourself becoming passionate about giving of yourself, your time and your resources to others as a result of volunteering or pursuing your most passionate of interests (more about this in Chapter Twelve).

You could make new acquaintances and new friends as a result, expanding your social circle. Best of all, these are most likely to be people of good and positive influence. They may include and invite you to participate in activities beyond the environment in which you first encountered them. By all means, make it known that you are single and interested in dating. You never known to whom you will be introduced, so accept any and all social invitations. The newfound energy you now generate has enormous potential to be attractive, charming and appealing to any number of potential prospects.

Chapter 4

A WORD ABOUT SOLUMATES

The concept of "star-crossed lovers" dates back to Shakespeare's *Romeo and Juliet* and probably before that. That people are destined or "fated" to meet and fall hopelessly in love is the stuff of epic romantic sagas. And may, indeed, grant hope for the prospect of meeting "Mr. Right" to those unsuccessful in love. The thought that the perfect mate is somewhere out there awaiting your discovery is certainly comforting as well as entirely possible. But is this what is meant when matchmakers and psychics talk about "soulmates"?

Soulmates suggest that two people are connected mentally-emotionally, physically and spiritually as divine partners on Earth because they are also metaphysically connected. This implies that there is a manifest-destiny due to both souls having been known to one another previously. As such, the idea is that they are acquainted in both the Heavenly realm, or Spirit dimension, but also over the course of many lifetimes together.

Not to burst any grandiose fantasy, but that's not necessarily a romantic suggestion. Knowing one another as soulmates over the course of any number of lifetimes *may* have romantic implications, but it may also reference heartbreak, tragedy, love lost or any variation of complex and complicated histories together. This is probably the more realistic interpretation of soulmates.

It is not incorrect to romanticize the idea of soulmates; but romanticize in the generic sense—as in a sweeping, thrilling and exhilarating ideal—instead of mad, passionate love. For example, there have been several instances in my psychic readings in which female clients have asked, "Why can't I seem to release my ex?" What this means is that they feel an inexplicable sense of duty, obligation or need to protect their former boyfriends and husbands to the point of distraction. This, in turn, prevents them from moving forward by engaging in a new relationship for always dropping everything to tend to the needs of the ex-partner, which can be exhausting.

The answer to *why* this happens more often than not is in keeping with the soulmate connection beyond this lifetime. This is why the relationship has been so confusing and exasperating—so many questions about the relationship are open-ended and unresolved! In these examples, what I have discovered is that there is, in fact, a past-life connection between my female clients and their former boyfriends or husbands. It is entirely fascinating to me, and eye-opening for my clients, because it puts everything into proper perspective for the first time.

In one instance in particular, I saw that the past life

connection was that my client was the mother of her old boyfriend, and he was her young son! The feeling I got was that this was during the late-1800s, as there was a saloon or possibly even a bordello involved. Yes, my client was a prostitute in that lifetime! I "saw" her in my mind's eye dressed in clothing of that era, but her costume was obviously provocative for the time. Additionally, the only women who would have been present in traditional "men's only" environments of the time period would be those of ill repute; "good girls" and women of class and pedigree would never frequent such establishments. Because of her circumstances, this client (as the prostitute) had little choice but to sell her own body. But doing so on a regular basis meant that she was often neglectful of her son, who spent a lot of time alone or in the company of unsavory characters. The shame and guilt and concern my client felt for her son carried over into the present day for the man whose soul had been her son *then*. This all rang true for my client who actually became emotional and tearful because, as she stated, "It all felt so familiar." (As a side note, it also provided her with a much-appreciated and much-needed explanation for her current-day promiscuity.)

In keeping with the soulmates-and-past-life theme, I have also intuited on any number of occasions that the reason why a great number of female clients are unable to "cut the cord" is—literally—precisely that. Once again, in a past lifetime, they were the mother and the ex-boyfriend or husband was the child they never knew *because they died during childbirth*. This rarely occurs anymore in modern times and in medically-equipped environments, but it was not an altogether unusual occurrence in eras past. There was a time when it was commonplace for women to give birth in their own homes because of the rural location, inability to afford medical care, or the general inaccessibility of a qualified doctor. This is why midwives were so prevalent; women who were experienced in assisting to birth babies outside of a hospital setting. Because of unforeseen complications, a healthy baby might be born but the birth mother hemorrhaged in the process, sacrificing her life for that of the child she would never come to know. And so, when these two souls meet again in the new context of a romantic relationship, detaching one's self from the soul who had been the "baby" is easier said than done.

I've also seen a similar scenario play out when the ex-boyfriend or husband is the reincarnated soul of a terminated pregnancy. As you are doubtless well aware, there have long been ongoing debates over a woman's right to choose what to do with her own body versus preserving what is defined as the fetus's right to life. Most often, the decision to terminate a pregnancy is not something done lightly or carelessly but with great consideration. Once again, in eras gone by, an abortion was not only shameful and disgraceful, it was also illegal. Because of this, non-professionals who had acquired the reputation for being skilled at this procedure were paid under the table. The environments in which the abortion took place were often unhygienic, even dangerous if the procedure were somehow botched. And so, not only did some women feel tremendous pressure and disgrace for pursuing the termination of their pregnancy, many also bled out as a result.

From a psychic perspective—and this may prove unpopular

and controversial with my conservative readers—the subject of terminating a pregnancy has been a non-issue. What this means is that I have been shown repeatedly that, ultimately, our souls never stray too far from the fold. There is no spiritual condemnation or shaming when this Earthly decision is made because nothing spiritual can ever be destroyed. What would have been the aborted soul uniformly comes back around to assume a role in the life of the pregnant mother, either as another child born under better circumstances; as a grandchild; or as a romantic partner. Given this latter contention, there is sometimes a lingering accountability experienced on the part of a female client who terminated the pregnancy at a time when there was great stigma associated with doing so. This residual effect from the prior lifetime makes it that much more difficult to release the present-day, former romantic relationship that is draining or even manipulative.

Finally, on more than a few occasions during a psychic session it has been revealed that the ex-boyfriend or former husband was, again, the son of my client. In these scenarios, however, the son is the eldest and first born, the sole male child or an only child, who went off to war and never came home. I have seen this applied to World War II, the Korean War and, more recently, the Vietnam War. Invariably, my clients validate that the former partner is, indeed, a war buff glued to the History Channel or YouTube video documentaries. Granting perspective on the emotional ties, and the "bleed-over" effect from a previous lifetime, has been emotionally healing for my clients. It has also provided them with the understanding and confidence to sever the ties that bind and cut the cord in old relationships in order to push onward.

As I stated, the concept of soulmates has been romanticized, perhaps unduly so. But did you know that your soulmate could be your own worst enemy? Again, it is more about the dynamic of the relationship and what is to be gleaned from it, and not just only about falling head-over-heels in love. Growing up in a very conservative era, my awkwardness and sensitivities made me an easy mark and a ready target once my peer group aged into adolescence and became more sophisticated and judgmental. In particular, one classmate made me his personal whipping boy and the object of his daily vexations, insults and physical harassment. This I endured every day of the school year for at least seven years. Not only was I verbally and physically abused, my speech and body language were openly mocked in front of adults who did little or nothing about it.

As you might imagine, because I rarely retaliated, others soon joined in, and I was most definitely odd-man out. Not only that, I became severely depressed to the point of suicidal ideation and I also developed what I know now to have been post-traumatic stress disorder. This was the darkest period of time in my life, and I nearly didn't survive it. But I did, through sheer will of endurance. In hindsight, now as an adult and one who has undergone self-analysis, I understand why this particular person was in my life. Believe it or not, I think there's a strong possibility that he is a soulmate of mine. There is much that I learned from the experience, including humility. Although I underwent a phase in which I became as cynical and unbearable as he was, I recognize now the worst traits to shed and shun. I was fortunate enough to have not only survived but to also have evolved; so far as I know, he is now a janitor in the same building at which we both attended high school. So, you see, it is possible to have more than one soulmate, multiple soulmates in fact. Of course, in my instance, romance didn't factor into the equation whatsoever.

A soulmate could also be your parent, grandparent, sibling or best friend. One of the most bittersweet examples of true soulmates, of which I am aware, started out as a loving romance that ended in divorce. The woman in question married her high school sweetheart and they had a son together. Some years later, her husband came out as gay. However, the bond was so solid that the lifelong friendship extended beyond the marriage breakup. They are in communication with one another nearly every day and still see each other regularly. Both have moved on romantically, but they remain inextricably bonded. I suspect the hows and the whys of this relationship will all be made crystal clear to them once they pass from this life to the next.

Finally, much has been made in recent years about another New Age romantic concept, that of "twin flames." There seems to be some confusion and overlap between the concepts of soulmates and twin flames. It might be argued that the examples I've given of soulmates may actually apply to twin flames. Popular thought is that twin flames are two halves of the same soul that are destined to find one another and unite in a moment of psychic knowingness and cosmic recognition. But is this deeper than merely a trendy template for hopeful singles?

As is true of soulmates, twin flames are not necessarily romantic partners. There is, though, a unifying energy between both individuals that correlates to similar life experiences, oftentimes nearly identical experiences. There is not only a feeling of familiarity during the introduction to the twin flame but a sense of unconditional understanding for having endured and survived very challenging, even traumatic, situations. Thus, the meeting of the twin flame may not be romantic so much as it is cathartic in nature. The union between both parties involves a tingling déjà vu-type of shared experiences that may prompt healing through addressing unresolved issues and coming to terms with long-denied truths. Undergoing this process may be draining and depleting for both parties.

Although twin flame relationships can be very intense, they may be entirely platonic. A lot may transpire within a compressed period of time, and like a flame, it may all burn brightly before extinguishing altogether. The closure of wounds that may be prompted by the twin flame relationship should be viewed as a short-term catalyst for positive change and spiritual growth. As a result, twin flames may or may not remain in close contact after the initial rush of commonalities is examined and exhausted. While this may be melancholy, it is not cause for alarm or anxiety. As with soulmates, it is possible to have more than one twin flame. In such case, it may be that the more seasoned of the two flames is able to serve as a mentor to the inexperienced half in the relationship.

Regardless of whether a romantic partner may be a soulmate or a twin flame, the very best romantic relationships begin as friendships. There is a great beauty that comes of a gradual merging through a variety of incidents and experiences that unifies, then solidifies, the friendship, paving the path for love to blossom. It is for this reason that I advise not to become caught up in overanalyzing if a new prospective partner is a soulmate, twin flame or remnant of a past-life relationship. Instead, focus your time, attention and energy of what you have in common with one another as well as what you might learn from one another by trying new experiences. This facilitates a unifying bond that can mature over time as both parties discover things about one another that are new revelations. This will be addressed in greater detail in Chapter Twelve.

Chapter 5

"I CAN FIX HIM"

The premise of many romantic comedies begins with two people of mismatched energy, in keeping with the old adage that opposites attract. There is something wistful to the idea of being "completed" or fulfilled by one who compensates for what the other lacks, such that one half of the couple complements the other. Just as was discussed in the previous chapter—that the best romances originate in friendships—so, too, may it be said that occasionally friction occurs before fondness, or at least that's how it happens in the movies. Personally speaking, I've had this occur a couple times, that I can recall, in non-romantic relationships; that is, people I started out really disliking actually became good friends. There's no reason why the same cannot be true of love connections.

But is it this notion—that opposites attract—that fuels those women who excuse or ignore the red flags and warning signs early on in a relationship that is doomed to fail? I have known women who see loving a flawed man as a personal challenge, but this is often tempered with a desperate desire to be needed. I'm not just talking about a man who has some random character flaws or a few social shortcomings that may be charming initially; I'm talking about men who are drug addicts, alcoholics, serial cheaters and those who are physically, sexually and psychologically abusive. And still she stays, just like the Pearl Jam song "Better Man," the lyrics of which paint a portrait of a woman who is too scared to leave an abusive relationship, so she surrenders, acquiesces and remains.

This type of scenario is a set-up ripe for manipulation by a male partner who is just along for the ride and will use and take as much as he can for having it so good. I have seen women in these kinds of romantic relationships and marriages who do everything for their partner, from cooking and cleaning to humiliating sex acts to caring for him as his health deteriorates. Because nothing is reciprocated, these women are clearly unhappy but will usually make excuses for their man's bad behavior, as though he were a child and not an adult. They don't want to be branded a quitter, nor do they want to feel like a failure for being unable to rehabilitate their man. They may not feel deserving of anything more. They want to belong and, so, create a fantasy that keeps lowering the bar in terms of what is tolerable. Bottom line is, they're willing to suffer in silence for not wanting to be alone. And, so, we come full circle to the themes of this book's very first chapter.

The most common male personality type in these types of situations is the narcissist. To a woman who is vulnerable and lacking in self-esteem or confidence, the narcissist can be irresistible—at first. He is suave and charming, and a smooth-talker who knows how to say all the right things to make a gal feel special and beautiful, as if she's the only person in the room. They may also, initially, be generous and accommodating, wanting only to please. But this fabricated façade cannot last forever; and anyone who has been in a relationship with a narcissist will tell you that they can be brilliant actors although there's always a tipping point in which they show their true selves (usually when their lies catch up with them).

Red flags for this personality type include a gradual shift away from the attention given to you so that they become the star attraction. The narcissist will frequently compliment himself, reminding others of his past achievements and referring to himself as a "genius." With a little research, it may be uncovered that these prior accolades are significantly embellished or flat-out fabricated altogether. The narcissist may also be truly good looking, but this has been reinforced often enough—and special accommodations have been granted because of such—that he is entitled and may refer to himself as a "stud." He may even brag about his sexual conquests but, like his academic or athletic achievements, this may be embellished or totally false. In fact, if you hesitate or do not comply with his sexual demands, he will quickly tell you how lucky you are because he can get his needs met elsewhere very easily. This may also morph into a very dangerous mentality if the narcissist is rejected, as in "If I can't have you, nobody will!"

Other toxic personality types include those with addictions of various sorts, ranging from drugs and alcohol to gambling and running up debt. Many women, who believe they are in love, will willingly enable the addictive personality by loaning or "floating" their male partner money upon request. Oftentimes, there are promises of repayment but that usually gets delayed or otherwise procrastinated. I'll never forget living in the same neighborhood as a successful woman psychologist. Her boyfriend didn't appear to work, and I'd often see him outside smoking a cigarette while waiting for her toy poodle to do its business. His eyes always looked sunken and lifeless, but he seemed friendly enough. One day, I caught him screaming at the dog when he thought no one was watching. He exuded extreme negative energy in that moment like I had not previously encountered. Shortly after that, several fires were set in a nearby construction-site trailer and a townhouse that was under construction. It was found that he was the arsonist, with a history of such activity, and he went to prison. Neighbors cleaning up the underbrush behind their home discovered dozens of empty liquor bottles that he had emptied and tossed back there. What was so surprising is that this woman, who was seemingly so intelligent and professional, had been deceived the entire time.

In another instance, a longtime client, who consulted with me on affairs of the heart, was also a very bright, well-educated and successful young gal. But when she came in for her last appointment, she was clearly distressed. I intuited that there as a serious division in a relationship directly connected to her. The soul energy of a very supportive grandfather came forward, saluting, as is my symbol for military service. The grandfather showed that she had tried to make the marriage work despite its rapid deterioration and in light of the grandfather referring to her husband as a "cheater." I was also able to intuit that her husband was addicted to alcohol and pornography, and that he probably had an undiagnosed mental illness. I also saw that in the heat of a recent argument, he actually called her the worst word by which anyone could refer to a woman, and she verified that, which is truly terrible. She had moved out and made the decision to divorce her husband. Part of her struggle was—as has been previously noted here—she didn't want to be a quitter; coming from a military family, it simply wasn't in her DNA. But she had to resign herself to the fact that the present state of the relationship was irreparable. She had been married less than two years.

So many women want to believe in the happily-ever-after fairy tale, that they overlook what objective outsiders would perceive as warning bells. So, from a spiritual perspective, why would this kind of situation occur to seemingly good, generous and intelligent women? As has been already noted, I have been shown repeatedly in psychic readings that toxic relationships are not time wasted if it was a learning opportunity (and some gals have to learn the lesson several times over before it sticks). I have been shown that knowing the worst of what a romantic relationship can be will embolden and empower, as well as aid, the person moving forward to know clearly the line between what she does want and what is not negotiable.

Oftentimes, the dissolution of a toxic relationship serves as a springboard of inspiration and ingenuity, leading to bolstered self-esteem and self-reliance. Many are the psychic sessions I've had with women who have rebounded in a manner that has propelled them to realize their hidden strengths and inner gifts, which had previously been dormant or undiscovered. Where new romance is concerned, I have also been shown another common theme: "This is not urgent, so don't be desperate."

The manifestation of negative energy in real time is among the warning bells of a toxic relationship that are metaphysical in nature. Oftentimes this type of manifestation is interpreted only as random incidents, separate from one another. The proper understanding is that they are, in fact, a collection of symptoms indicating an overall syndrome of spiritual siege. People in unhappy, abusive relationships can attest to the gradual intrusion of a heavy, pervasive gloom and a disruption to the quality of their lives. The nature of very dark energy is to stealthily infiltrate the environment so gradually that it is barely detectable over time. Not only is the mental-emotional health of the individuals concerned seriously affected, literally so is the physical living space itself.

When the influence of negative energy starts to spill over into real time, the following collection of symptoms may be indicators of its presence:

- Sleep disturbances, including the onset, or worsening, of insomnia, nightmares and night terrors for any household member.

- Problems with electricity including malfunctioning appliances, light bulbs frequently blowing, computers scrambling and crashing, and devices turning on and off by themselves or changing channels.

- Household pets reacting to, or "tracking," something unseen. Cats may hiss and dogs may bark. They may resist entering a particular room that is the seat of a lot of the activity.

- Small objects may go missing, such as a set of keys, and resurface in places that are illogical (like a bathroom drawer) or were previously searched.

- The sensation of being watched, especially in the bathroom or while showering.

- Catching something moving out of the corner of one eye, or actually seeing shadow-shaped figures.

- The abusive person's behavior may intensify, becoming violent or despondent to the point of threatening harm to himself or others.

If you have lived through such circumstances—or you are currently dealing with this kind on onslaught—take heart in knowing that there is a remedy to contain it. No, I'm not talking about holy water, sage or crystals (not that I'm discouraging of their use either). Nothing trumps the supreme power of your heartfelt prayers and setting of positive, proactive intentions. Call in the troops, be it whatever you call the Higher Power; your angels; deceased loved ones; or religious figures such as saints, if you wish. Bless your own living environment, with the assistance and support of any other household member, or close friend, who wishes to unite forces with you as an ally in this mission. If an addictive, abusive personality resides in the same household, then the blessing of your own living environment will not be once and done. It will need to be cleansed on a weekly basis until it is noticeable that symptoms have subsided if not dissipated altogether.

At the least, visualize creating a protective barrier around your own bedroom and that of others who are being negatively affected. In your mind's eye, picture a glorious golden shield of luminous light over the room. Lift up your arms to draw it near to you and, extending your reach, motion with your arms so that the shield of luminous light covers above, around and finally, below you, creating a beautiful bubble. This shield will insulate and incapsulate; it will defend and protect; and it will repel and deflect anything that is not for the greater good of the highest order. You may use this exact language, or your own version of it; but know that there is no single, specific prayer or blessing to say, and if it is all heart-centered, you cannot fail to enact it all correctly.

Some women attempt to terminate a bad relationship but have a difficult time saying "no," especially when it comes to intimacy. The lure of great sex with an ex can be enticing if not intoxicating; both parties know each other very well and know one another's likes and dislikes, so there's no awkwardness or guesswork. This arrangement is almost always a bad idea. Firstly, because during sex there's a blending and braiding of energy that is exchanged between both parties. So, you are defeating the purpose of eradicating negative energy if you persist in granting it permission to attach! And, as countless women have discovered, being "friends with benefits" just doesn't work.

Men can compartmentalize and see sex as just sex, detached from emotional ties; women don't usually think this way for associating emotion with the sexual encounter. This may give hope to rehabilitating a broken relationship when, in fact, it is a relationship of convenience. Adult film performer Jenna Jameson, whose job it was to have sex with a number of male partners, has stated that it was "hard not to have feelings about some of the actors I worked with…How can you do all this stuff with these guys and then feel nothing for them?" I wish I had a dollar for every time a deceased father or ex-partner came through in a psychic reading and explained, "I didn't take my dick with me," meaning that absent their genitals and the male sex drive, they were granted a whole new perspective on their own behavior which was eye-opening.

In concluding this chapter, please understand that a primary priority is to your own mental-emotional, physical and spiritual well-being so that you are in the best possible position to be attracting healthy romantic energy. There's certainly nothing wrong with desiring to help someone who is having a rough time but be smart about it. Set limits and boundaries based on the behavior you have observed. And know that a broken person is not your science project. What this means is that it is not your place to take on someone ailing or addicted as your personal mission to transform him into the person you believe he has potential to become. Yes, people can, and do, change. The key to an authentic transformation, however, is they have to want it. And they, and they alone, must be willing to completely confront the truth by taking full and personal responsibility.

– Chapter 6 –

TRUST YOUR PETS

You may not realize it but, if you are a pet owner, you may well have the most intuitive and devoted ally right under your very nose. Your pet wants to be of service to you in reciprocation for all that you have offered him or her, particularly if that animal is a rescue. Those pets tend to be the most grateful and appreciative of all. This I know, for having had a long history of communicating with animals—usually dogs—and for having written a book all about those experiences.

The first time I communicated with a living creature, it happened quite by surprise and rather spontaneously. No, I was not a small child but an adult in my forties! I was getting ready to relax with a book in my sunroom and, because it was such a balmy day, decided to open the sliding glass door and expose the screen door for a little cross-ventilation breeze. As I did so, I noticed a Praying Mantis was struggling to climb up the vinyl siding on the exterior of the room, just outside the door. I thought I'd try being helpful, so I quickly located a sturdy twig and extended it to the Mantis as an alternative to the slippery siding. To my surprise, it accepted the twig and climbed aboard. I carried the twig and Mantis to the far end of my backyard and set it down in the underbrush of the sloping hillside.

Once on the ground, the Mantis slowly disembarked, and I was struck by how it moved in such a stately and graceful manner. But my admiration clouded over when I realized the Mantis had wasted no time in grabbing hold of a passing beetle and, with an audible crunching, was consuming the smaller insect alive! A bit repulsed, I turned away. When I looked back, the Mantis was finishing its meal and, I swear, it turned and looked directly at me. I "heard" in my head, "Would you have me eat something already dead?" I was taken aback; I certainly hadn't expected to engage with this unusual creature but, when I thought about it, its position on cannibalism made sense to me as very few creatures are scavengers of carrion. And, I suppose, if you don't know where your next meal is coming from, you take it where you can get it!

The encounter with the Praying Mantis made me realize that I had the potential to be interacting similarly with any living creature. (Curiously enough, I had always regarded Mantises as supremely intelligent, so perhaps my initiation was no coincidence.) Thereafter, I began to interact with neighborhood dogs while out on my daily strolls. The dogs were being walked by their owners, but I found that they were now more likely to be open to my approaching them. At first, I tried to be discreet, but I became too anxious to receive confirmation of what they were sharing with me. So, I started to inquire of their owners the specifics that were being posed to me by the clever canines. Random thoughts confided in me were that of missing a teenage daughter who had gone off to college to complaining that the numerous air fresheners in the household were exacerbating an already compromised respiratory system. I also found that the way I received intuitive information from the dogs was precisely the same as if I were interacting with a human client during a psychic reading. That is, it all came through as an extension and magnification of my own senses.

Unlike us, animals are not socially conditioned to disbelieve things that are mystical and mysterious. As a result, they have no preconceived notions and no filters. They just experience life in the moment as it unfolds with little regard for the past or the future. This is why pet owners will often report to me that they believe their dog or cat is "psychic." I believe that the animals can sense spiritual energy visiting or passing through, and that they "track" its motion by turning their head to "watch" something that, to everyone else, is unseen. This may very well be harmless, if not even playful; and the pets' reactions are out of curiosity or perhaps indifference (to them, spiritual energy isn't much different than interacting with you or I). Similarly, it is dogs or cats that tend to be extra sensitive to any negative energy that may be intruding upon one's living environment. This manifests when they refuse to go into a certain room for very long (or not at all), or urinate in that room out of fear, anxiety or to send a warning communication of marking turf. The animals may also bark or hiss at something no one else is able to see as well. This, too, is a warning to untoward energy to stay out and keep away.

Given this hypersensitivity, it is important to recognize that your animal's intuition is a valuable commodity and is to be trusted. Animals tend to have an innate ability to see people's energy fields, or auras, which radiate around them and extend outwardly from the physical form. When an animal reacts positively or negatively to someone upon first meeting them, it may be because they are responding to the sensation and color being emitted from a person's auric field. Obviously, if someone is genuine and sincere, their aura will project a warmth that matches the color of the aura, which may be bright white, yellow or pastel colors. Conversely, a narcissist may give off energetic vibes that are confusing or untrustworthy and may generate colors that portend the truth of their personality: angry reds, muddy browns, desolate grays and, of course, black. The negative personality may also have visible (to the animal) holes or tears in their auric field due to harm and destruction to others and one's self. Because of this, household pets can be an excellent judge of character, which will be a particularly useful tool when it comes to confirming, or contradicting, your own first impressions of a romantic relationship.

As affirmation of this, more than one client has told me, "If he doesn't like my pet, he doesn't pass the litmus test." These are obviously very smart gals for putting their devotion to their animals ahead of any would-be beau! And who wouldn't? Well, you might also be surprised at the number of clients who have told me of the sacrifices they have made to appease the new man in their life by selling or giving away their animals. It's hard to imagine, but that's how a desperate mind operates, by rationalizing priorities based on the need to be needed instead of heeding the red flags being communicated by their pets. The women that opt for this approach tend to be numb to their own intuition, such that their good judgement is clouded. But these are precisely the people who should be giving more credence to the ability of their pets to serve as good guides in determining who to trust. As one such example, recall the anecdote from the last chapter of the neighbor who was being duped by the boyfriend who turned out to be an arsonist. Around her and her dog, he was sweetness and light—with the exception of the sole circumstance in which he let down his guard and, unbeknownst to him, I observed him screaming at the dog when he thought he was alone.

What the average person doesn't realize is that our pets are extraordinarily spiritual. Think about it: None of them speak and they live their lives in a perpetual meditation, always thinking, sensing, living in the moment. Who else lives like this other than animals? The human equivalent would be individuals of elevated religious appointment such as the nun, the monk, the yogi, the guru, the priest, the shaman or the rabbi. These people spend absorbing amounts of time in meditative silence throughout each day. They do this in order to go within themselves and connect with the essence of our collective Source. The stronger the connection, the greater the understanding and knowingness. I can tell you that, personally speaking, my psychic gifts enhanced and strengthened exponentially as a result of tuning in, as in this manner. Well, our pets are naturally born into a similar state of being. For them, being attuned to spiritual energy and guidance is as natural as breathing. Their ability to discern our collective existence in this world is more finely developed than most human beings.

Rescue animals are, in particular, oftentimes very loyal and devoted to their caretakers. They understand that their very lives were saved from an early termination by your compassionate intervention. But it is not unusual for a pet owner to report, "She picked me, I didn't pick her" or "He found me by accident." This is never coincidence, rest assured. I can attest to this myself. When I went to select my puppy some years ago, she clearly picked me as she pushed her way over her kennelmates to place herself front and center in my line of vision. If any of her cohabitants tried to join her, she snapped at them, and they backed away. Then she went back to smiling, tongue hanging out and tail wagging. Clearly, she had loads of personality but, as I later learned, she could match me in her stubbornness and determination to be right.

Additionally, our pets have spiritual stations, or roles, assigned to them. This assignment occurs prior to them incarnating into this world, same as us. As such, they bring exactly what is needed to our lives and our homes because it has all already been preordained. For example, some animals are protectors and guardians. I have had dogs "show" me psychically that they would fight to the death, if necessary, in order to defend a family member. Others have swelled up their chests to show me a pretend sheriff's badge pinned to them, indicating that they are the chief of police whose job it is to patrol the home and grounds from pests and intruders. Some animals are nurses and nannies, caregivers for a new baby or young children. In exceptional instances, these animals have saved young children from harm or alerted others to a threatening danger. The station of comedian is one that is commonplace, usually in households that require something to balance the tension or emotional conflict. I recall one little Lhasa Apso named Daisy who was so funny looking that she made me laugh every time I saw her. Daisy had a tough lot as her owners frequently argued and drank, most of which I could hear just by standing on the sidewalk outside their house.

The most reverential station for a pet is that of healer. As is true of the other positions, most people are totally oblivious to how very hard their animals are working to fulfill their dutiful obligations. The healing pet has been assigned to an owner, or owners, who are struggling with their mental-emotional or physical well-being. These are the animals that not only try to comfort and soothe by de-stressing us after a long day, they literally are physicians of a kind. Have you ever had a cat or dog put its head on you in the exact place on your body where you were hurting? I've had clients report that their cat will wrap itself around their head when they are resting and, upon rising, their headache or migraine has been relieved. What's happening here? I'll tell you as the animals have shown it to me.

Believe it or not, when they lay on you or against you, they are siphoning energetic toxins from your body in an effort to heal you. Sometimes a dog will get in close and press the entire length of her torso up against her owner in order to facilitate this process. But what happens to the toxins? Where do they go? Here's the most heart-wrenching, amazing and altruistic aspect of the whole thing: These animals are deliberately absorbing the toxic energy into their own bodies at the risk of causing harm and damage to themselves, knowing it may end their own life prematurely. Now that's sacrifice.

And I've had many animals show me, in psychic visions, that they were preparing to die long before anyone else knew or before a terminal diagnosis was made. They are peaceful and serene about the process, for having experienced it many times before. They don't think of death as a finality, they think in terms of ongoing cycles of life. They are more concerned for us than they are about themselves. They have consistently shown me the same symbolic imagery: A sky at dusk streaked with hues of coral, yellow and orange that slowly fades to black as the sun sets behind the horizon.

Perhaps as a result of the depth of this understanding, you may newly appreciate the significance of paying keen attention to how your pets act and react around people to whom you introduce them. They know best and want what's best for us. First impressions matter. If you introduce a male romantic partner to your dog or cat, watch for how the animal behaves. Also pay attention to how the man responds as well. If the animal appears indifferent, or runs and hides, be patient and see if she reemerges after a period of becoming acclimated to your friend's presence and the sound of his voice. It may not happen the first time out either; but you would recognize if this was typical conduct or unusual behavior after the second or third attempt to engage. If it persists—and you truly believe your friend is kind and decent—encourage him to make a peace offering by feeding your pet at meal time, or gifting your pet with some special food treat, so that the animal will be more likely to come out of their shell and show a trust for associating the food with your friend.

Be mindful, too, that older animals tend to be wiser and more seasoned. So, if you have more than one animal, you may notice that the younger pets are more carefree and oblivious. They may, in fact, seem very receptive and affectionate. They may be more openly gregarious in greeting your male companion, licking, kissing and jumping up excitedly. But pay careful attention to the manner in which the elder animals behave, as this will probably be most telling of all. If the older pets seem cautious and reserved, preferring to observe at a distance, accept that they are taking their time by sizing him up and not rushing to judgement.

An animal that growls and tries to bite at first introduction is sending a very clear communication of being defensive and distrusting. Its hair may bristle, and it may tremble with trepidation. The reason for this could be threefold. First, it may just be that the animal's station is protector, which means he or she is being vigilant in carrying out the duty of assignment in loyalty to you. (If you've been single for some time, there could be an element of jealousy that comes to bear upon this stance as well.) Should you sense this too, simply have a private chat with your pet—at a later, calmer date and time—in which you communicate how much you thank and appreciate him or her for their good efforts, and that you recognize what they are doing for you. Explain that your male friend is a good person and someone whom you like, and it is okay for your pet to assist you in making him feel welcome in your home. Your pet may not comprehend every word of what you are saying, but I promise they will feel and sense the emotions with which you are saying it. And that is what will resonate within them. It will require some internal reorganization on their part, and probably a gentle reminder just before your date visits next, but you should see improved relation between the two.

Second, your pet may be responding to your male friend defensively because the man has triggered a traumatic memory from the past. Yes, it is possible for animals to suffer from post-traumatic stress disorder the same as human beings. Most often, I have found, is that animals (especially rescues) are frightened and intimidated by men who have loud, masculine voices, who laugh too raucously, move too suddenly, smell a certain way (like smoke or alcohol), or even wear certain colors or types of clothing, such as a uniform. Their reaction, which may seem like an overreaction, is clearly due to having been abused by someone that reminds them of your male friend. If you suspect this to be true, and you will likely know this from previous experience, then you will understand the importance of taking time and patience to develop the relationship incrementally, meaning baby steps. If your boyfriend is a good person, he will put forth the effort to bond with your pet by making compassionate accommodations. (If he is really stellar, he'll do this intuitively and without you even having to broach the subject.) This means that he will change his approach and demeanor in order to gradually create a comfort level and a mutual feeling of trust with your pet. His demonstration and willingness to do this should say a lot of about him and the future of the relationship.

Third, and finally, if your animal continually responds very strongly and in a negative way to your male companion, it may well be because he or she is picking up on something that you are not. In the worst-case scenario, the animal is actually reacting to the monstrous form in which the negative energy of the man has taken shape and attached to his person. If you are in the throes of the initial stages of a courtship, then you are both on your best behavior during this "honeymoon phase" of the relationship. Again, if you have been lonely and dateless for quite some time, then you are likely to be in "pleaser" mode, desiring to be as easy and comfortable to be with as possible. Your pet isn't interested in pleasing anyone else but you, so they have no hidden agenda; what you see is what you get.

Your being smitten may also cause you to be romantically deaf and blind to what is painfully obvious to your pet. In fact, your pet may try to clue you in on this by behaving in an especially bratty way. If your animal urinates on, or bites, rips or destroys, a personal item belonging to your boyfriend, that's a pretty salient communication along the lines of, "Here's what I think of you!" It's the same as your pet giving him the middle finger if they possessed the dexterity to do so. If this behavior persists, or even worsens, it is a warning to you. If your male friend reacts to any of these behaviors adversely by yelling, swearing at, swatting, pushing or even outright hitting your pet, it is grounds for termination of the relationship. It could very well also be an indication of what's in store for you if you don't.

Bottom line is, if your male partner doesn't try to make friends with your animal companions, it may be very telling for your romantic future with him. By all means, pay attention. Be unafraid to talk about it with your pet. Ask their advice (really!).

They'll show you what they're thinking through their actions and behavior. Again, they may not fully understand every word of what you are saying, but they will certainly feel it enough to process it internally and give it careful consideration. If you have a symbiotic relationship with your pet, this process will be one of trusting support and loving collaboration. Prior to reading this chapter, you may not have realized that one of your greatest champions and dearest allies has been living under the same roof with you, under your very nose and hiding in plain sight. But now you know.

Chapter 7

GO YOUR OWN WAY

"I'm so confused and upset," said my twenty-something client, "I don't know what to do! I love him but I don't think my family will approve of him or even like him. What do I do?" This young woman's dilemma was, unfortunately, not unusual and her plea for direction is commonplace in my line of work as a psychic medium. Her situation was that she had fallen in love with a young man who was of another race and culture other than her own and that of her family. Knowing her family to be very conservative, she feared the potential repercussions of rejection, estrangement and disownment should she make the relationship public.

Of course, romance with someone that meets with family disapproval for being "from the wrong side of the tracks," or from a different social class, are part and parcel of the human condition since time immemorial. Our religious beliefs, genetic heritage or the color of one's skin have given rise to all forms of hatred here on Earth for centuries. Just when we think we've made strides in improvement, some event occurs to set things back, and we realize we're beginning virtually all over again. It is an issue peculiar to being human. And just like all those unfaithful deceased ex-husbands and fathers who confessed that, absent their male organs, they had an entirely new perspective in the Spirit World, so, too, is the appearance of our human form of no consequence there either.

When we take our last breath and transition to the Heavenly Realm, we release all rights to the physical form that once housed us temporarily. Think of it in the same way as you would when leasing a car; it is yours for the duration of the lease agreement but once the contract expires, so does your claim to ownership of the property. The same is true of our physical form. Now, this may be disturbing to some readers who may worry with anxiety over losing their identity. If this is your concern, let me put you at ease: We don't. You will still be you. You will still recognize your own thoughts and feelings, but all of this will be magnified and expanded in the most delightful, exhilarating way.

I can say this with confidence because I have experienced it myself. Most significantly, I once had a vivid dream in which I encountered an invisible barrier in my own home that blocked me from entering my living room. Sensing it had been placed there as a test, my objective was to find a way to circumvent the invisible barrier and still get to where I needed to be. I happened to notice a small hole in the wall of the barrier, a miniscule crevice. In my mind, I transformed myself into a liquid state and, like a fluid ribbon, slipped right through the hole and came out the other side unscathed—mission accomplished! My point is sharing this anecdote is that I clearly recall the sensation of being liquid, but my identity was not altered in any way. I was still me.

The same sensation is true in the Heavenly Realm. We leave our human form behind in favor of returning to a state of pure energy. Think of it as if you are a single note on a musical scale. You vibrate at a specific frequency that is the sound the note makes, but you also become a color that corresponds to the note. You are entitled to occupy the note on the scale, although the entire musical composition would be incomplete absent your note. As we all have free will as human beings, so does our soul have free will as well; your musical note can be adjusted in color and vibration based on what you contribute to it. It may grow dim and quiet when contemplating or meditating, or it may explode in fireworks of joyous rapture. If you outwardly shimmer as a color and frequency, you may be wondering how you'll recognize your loved ones or how they'll recognize you. Simple: As a compassionate accommodation for one another, we can project an image of the appearance by which we'd best remember our soul in human form. This may only be necessary upon first returning to our Heavenly Home and until we get reacquainted with the routine once again. We will otherwise know one another by identifying the vibration of frequency and color, like how you unexpectedly hear an old, favorite song and it not only makes you feel good, it also conjures thoughts and emotions you associate in memory with that tune.

The purpose in explaining all of this is that when you are torn between your true love and the wishes of your family (or your fear of their reaction to your boyfriend), understand that it is all very temporary. In the Spirit World, we are no longer in human form, with two arms, two legs, two eyes, and so on. There is no bias, no prejudice based on one's background or skin color. Plus, once we get to the Heavenly Realm and reflect back on our lifetime, it will all seem as though it flashed by very quickly and in the blink of an eye. Is it really worth denying yourself happiness with someone whom you believe is the love of your life in order to keep the peace within your family? This sacrifice is a false equivalency when compared against the anxiety over the disapproval of others, including parents.

It may also well be that your relationship with someone else, which breaks from tradition, serves as a spiritual test and a teachable moment for others. A white female client was expressing concern about introducing her black boyfriend to her very conservative family, even though the couple was becoming quite serious. In particular, her father had some longstanding, prejudiced beliefs. Through me, Spirit encouraged her to proceed as planned. It was even foretold that, one day, we will eventually all blend to become the same café au lait color, so the color of our skin is ultimately inconsequential. Thus, it may be that your romantic relationship serves a twofold purpose. Not only is it a love connection for you, it may also support others in understanding the themes of unconditional love, acceptance, selflessness and evolution.

Interestingly enough, these fundamental contentions arose in the midst of a psychic reading I was giving a young woman of Turkish descent who was strongly considering engagement with a young man whom she was seeing. The challenge for her was that her beau was not Turkish and becoming engaged to him would break from longstanding family tradition. During the course of her session, her deceased Turkish grandmother began communicating to her through me. The grandmother had been very much "old school" when it came to upholding family customs and traditions. She even mentioned certain dishes that were her culinary specialty. But, in the Heavenly Realm, grandma had clearer vision for what matters and what is most important.

My client's grandmother spoke of her own marriage, which had been arranged—something my client confirmed. She said that it was very difficult to attempt to find love with someone with whom she didn't feel a strong emotional bonding, unlike my client's situation with her boyfriend. Grandma was caring but firm in communicating the importance of not looking back with regret, one day, for the relationship her granddaughter was afraid to have in the present. "You have to go your own way," was how my client's grandmother summarized it. I thought it was sound advice; but just as quickly, I saw the grandmother throw back both hands in the air. This is my symbol to convey to me their "hands off" policy. What this means is that our loved ones in Spirit can offer suggestions, provide recommendations and portray a vision for what the future may hold; but it is not their place to—nor would they want to— impose upon anyone's free will. In essence, what my client's grandmother was saying was, "I lived in a time when my romantic aspirations were suppressed and denied. You can't live your life just to please other people. But you must make your own decisions." In other words, grandma was not telling my client what to do but was encouraging her to consider her options carefully.

This is similar to the countless deceased mothers, grandmothers and great aunts whom I have channeled over the years who come forward to contrast the era in which they lived their lives with those of my clientele. Specifically, they have expressed their support for their loved one who is unhappy in a relationship. If it is a situation that seems repairable, they will sometimes say, "Do you think I was jumping up and down with joy every moment of my marriage? It's a compromise of give and take." This type of statement may be very surprising to someone who, as a child, idealized the older female's marriage but was not privy to any behind-the-scenes turmoil. This perspective may be a tad disillusioning but it is intended to be a motivation to fix what is fixable, and to seek resources such as therapy or marriage counseling.

Additionally, wise female ancestors in Spirit often point out that women of their time didn't readily have divorce as a choice because of social or religious stigma attached to it. They suggest that my female clientele are not obligated to endure abusive or unhappy relationships in the way that many women of prior eras often did. The message has consistently been one of stressing that life is too short to waste time enduring a situation where love is unfulfilled. It is not fair to either party, actually. Again, the ancestors are not dictating or prescribing what is to be done. Those who remained in unhappy marriages will usually show how it affected them as a way of providing a lesson based on experience. Some became severely depressed, turned to alcohol to cope, or drifted into affairs.

Others tolerated their husband's bad behavior but were determined to make their own happiness. This they did by pursuing hobbies and avocations, such as taking up painting, cooking classes or ballroom dancing. They found fulfillment by volunteering their time to various charitable organizations, helping others. They surrounded themselves with female friends with whom they could take day trips and in whom they could confide. And they cultivated relationships with others that resulted in "chosen family," meaning people who became like kin because of the close bond. These relationships became so gratifying that they compensated for the manner in which these women detached and grew apart from their husbands emotionally.

So, you see, the concept of going your own way doesn't just pertain to remaining true to the man with whom you've fallen in love. It's not necessarily about bucking the family hierarchy in favor of an elopement or shotgun wedding. It's also about the oftentimes heartbreaking decision whether to stay in an unhappy relationship or a loveless marriage that's soured over time. You may not have yet developed enough confidence in your own personal intuition to determine a viable course of action about separation or divorce. Or possibly you are anxious about your family disapproving of someone to whom you have become fondly devoted. If this applies to you, what may be helpful is to receive reinforcing validation of your own thoughts and feelings and intuition by consulting a reputable psychic or psychic medium.

Locating someone authentic might start with asking close friends or trusted coworkers if they know of anyone. Positive word of mouth is the best endorsement and has, for me, been the single greatest opportunity for booking referrals. If there is someone within driving distance from you who comes highly recommended, investigate further what is involved and how to book an in-person appointment. If there is no one local to you, there are plenty of psychics who practice exclusively online using a video-chat platform or by phone consultation. Be certain you know what type of person you'll be working with, as psychics and psychic mediums are two different things. A psychic can give you intuitive guidance about any aspect of your life, be it employment, relocation, travel, your children, your pets and, of course, romance. A psychic medium can do all that but can also tap into the soul energy of your deceased loved ones who are in Spirit. If you feel as if you wish for advice from the loving essence of your dearly departed, the latter professional is whom you should seek out. But know that highly gifted psychic mediums are in great demand and, so, they may come with a fee to match that demand in addition to a long waitlist. If you can't afford it and you can't wait, there is an alternative that is along the lines of "do it yourself." It is a process you can undergo in the privacy of your own home and won't cost you a cent, which leads us to the next chapter.

Chapter 8

SPIRITUAL GUIDANCE

Believe it or not, you have at your immediate disposal a myriad of spiritual allies and resources who desire to assist you and want to see you succeed in your aspirations. You can access these beneficent aides on-demand and in the manner of a psychic medium. Better yet, the likelihood of your receiving loving confirmation in this way is actually a greater possibility than were you to consult a psychic medium. This is due to the fact that your relationship with these allies and resources is very intimate, personal and specific to you!

There are several entities, or energies, if you will, that are at your service and awaiting your invitation to collaborate. The first is, of course, the most supreme of all and that is the source of our very creation. This energy has many names and is most commonly called God. But in recent times, there has been a shift away from use of the word God, as was mentioned previously (perhaps because for some it holds religious connotations). It matters not what you call it, just so long as you acknowledge this presence as you would a protective parent or older sibling that has your best interests at heart. From this source, all others emanate and serve as ambassadors on behalf of it, and on behalf of all that is right and true and good and kind.

Did you know you have a best friend you forgot you had? This friend was a comrade and mentor when you were a soul in the Heavenly Realm. Prior to your birth, you and this friend entered into a sacred pact. The agreement was that your friend would serve and support you behind the scenes while you live out your human existence. Just like Jiminy Cricket in Pinocchio, the friend's intention is to become a glorified version of your own conscience, trying to keep you on the straight and narrow path; to distract your attention to the people, places and things that will serve your greater good; and to act as a muse to impress inspiration within you. Once you are born, you will develop an amnesia about most everything that transpired in Heaven, although some of us will have fleeting recall as very young children. Others among us may have even interacted with this friend early on in the form of an "imaginary playmate." I have asked certain female clients if they remember making mud pies with an imaginary playmate or having a pretend tea party with him or her. When they enthusiastically admit "yes," I share with them that the playmate was, in fact, not imaginary and has been with them always. This presence is called your Spirit Guide.

Your Spirit Guide doesn't have to remain in the

background, relegated to the backstage of your life experience. But, with the exception of extreme emergencies, your Spirit Guide and other spiritual helpers, will not interfere with your free will and will therefore not insert themselves where they don't belong. That is, unless you invite them in! The procedure for doing this is very simple and uncomplicated. First step is to get yourself alone in a quiet space, free from distractions and interruptions. That means, power off everything. Say a prayer or a blessing to ensure that you are surrounded by love and protection (there is no particular prayer or special words, just whatever comes from your heart). Consider the role of your Spirit Guide in your life, as a counselor and mentor. Try to sense if your Guide is male or female or, perhaps, if your Guide is some other living creature such as an animal or a bird.

Next, christen your Spirit Guide with a name of your own choosing. It may be a name you've always liked the sound of. It may be a name you eliminated as a name for one of your children or pets. It may the first name that pops into your head or you may feel it came to mind in an unusual or mysterious way. In any case, select the name and say out loud, "I christen thee _____, and I give you permission to come forward. I invite you to make your presence known and to take a more active role in my life as my partner and collaborator." You may adjust the language to make it your own, of course. And that's it! There's no prolonged ritual, no pretentious ceremony of any kind. But, just like any friendship, you'll get out of it what you put into it. Remember, this is a partnership.

That doesn't mean that you now sit back and let your Spirit Guide do all the work and then bitterly complain when things don't work out in your favor. You have to be conscious and aware of connecting and communicating with your guide on a regular basis, even if only to offer gratitude for their loving support. You wouldn't text message someone you just met and ask them to run errands for you, would you? That would not only be extremely awkward and uncomfortable, it would be socially inappropriate. Apply this mindset to the relationship with your Guide, same as you do with God.

Many people whom I have counseled have discovered that about a week to ten days after christening their Guide, they have received validation of the presence in real time. This is precisely what happened to me when I named my Guide "Frank." One week later, my doorbell rang and standing there was a young man who had been driving the garbage pickup truck that day. He came to tell me that when he was backing out of my cul-de-sac, he clipped my mailbox post and split it. I asked if the sanitation company would pay for a replacement. He said they would, and he handed me the contact information; but when I looked at the slip of paper he had handed me, it was his name and number. "I thought you said they'd pay for a replacement post," I asked. Then it dawned on me, "Oh, if I report this does that put you in any jeopardy?" He said it would affect his driving record and that he would just as soon purchase the replacement post himself and return to install it. I told him I would consider his offer and we parted ways.

Within the hour, I had decided to honor this young man's honesty. As I processed what had occurred, I realized that he could have driven off and I wouldn't have known a thing, as I never heard a sound. When I went to call him, not only was his name Frank, the name of my Guide, his last name was Ward. That stuck in my head for about twenty-four hours as if something was nudging me. I finally understood that "ward" was a word in the English language. I pulled out my dictionary and was pleasantly surprised to learn that the definition of the word ward pertains to guardianship and the act of keeping guard! This young man's name translated to "Frank the Guardian"! Frank Ward did, indeed, make good on his promise to replace my mailbox post and as he was switching out the old post for the new one he had bought, he told me that he was never meant to be there the day of the accident; he was filling in for someone who had called out sick, it was his first time driving in the area and his regular route was a good twenty-five miles away!

There could be no denying the extraordinary synchronicity of this event. Now—and to be clear—Frank Ward is not my Spirit Guide! However, his name was a symbolic way of affirming the presence of my Frank, which was the intent of the communication. This is how Spirit operates, kind of like playing a game of charades. If you are conscious and aware, you will be notified, through signs and symbols, what is being conveyed from the Other Side. Once you christen your Spirit Guide, you may not receive a validation as spectacular as my own, as in the form of a name. Instead, the validation of your Guide's presence may coincide with your noticing a greater frequency of synchronicities, such as seeing triple digits on clocks, or reading a word at the same time someone says the same word or feeling a moment of creative inspiration that makes you feel as though the idea wasn't entirely your own. You may also notice that when you think of your Guide, you see a flash of blue light or get a temporary ringing in one ear that passes quickly, almost as if the energy in the room has shifted frequency. Again, this should all occur within a week to ten days of christening your Spirit Guide.

If you feel as though you haven't received a validation of your Spirit Guide's presence, try the process again, or try using a different name with which to christen your Guide. It's a bit like naming a new pet; the very first name you chose may not be the name that sticks in favor of a nickname or another name altogether. Heck, that evens happens with some people who go by a nickname instead of their given name because they prefer it or because others have called them a name that stuck over time, such as "Red," for their ginger hair, or "Butch," or "Buddy."

Pay attention and be aware of any uptick in your consciousness that draws your attention to enhanced opportunities. Pay attention to whatever may cause the flow of your day to run smoothly and in your favor. Try to recall whatever fragments of your dreams you can recollect during this period (more on dreams in the following chapter). These could all be indicators of a heightened sense of awareness that is in keeping with your Spirit Guide's high-vibration frequency. What this means is that you are tuning in to that frequency and tapping into the Divine in a manner more conscious than ever before. You should also notice that mentally-emotionally and physically you feel "lighter," meaning happier and less likely to worry about things beyond your control. This is a good thing as what you are projecting will affect your entire demeanor, making you more attractive as you are perceived by others. Your connectivity is precisely what will set the stage for romantic attraction of a caliber in keeping with that of your own.

It is wonderful to know you have a spiritual ally in your Spirit Guide, but there are others who wish to support you as well. In addition to your lead, or primary Guide, you may have additional Guides who step forward from time to time. The more you become attuned, the more you will know the difference between the energetic sensation associated with your primary Guide and the feelings you get when a different Guide is present. Each Guide will have a variation in rhythm of frequency and personality which may contrast with that of the others. For example, your lead Guide could present as a serious, old-fashioned "schoolmarm" type if you are in need of self-discipline and help with prioritizing. But a supplementary Guide could be playful, humorous and perhaps even a bit mischievous. Yet another Guide might be focused on family matters and may have more of a maternal-, paternal- or sibling-based energy.

Still others may have as their area of expertise an acumen for which you are lacking, such as confidence in social settings or an ability for financial savviness. Where you are and what's going on in your life will determine which of your group or team is likely to step forward. And if you aren't sensing them, then put out the call and make the request. They know enough about the human experience to understand how to collaborate with you and will attempt to honor your requests. But, remember, they do not interfere with free will and are awaiting your invitation to become involved.

Aside from a partnership with at least one Spirit Guide, you also have at your disposal a cadre of ethereal Guardians. What's the difference between the two, you might wonder? Remember, a Spirit Guide is not someone you have known in human form in your current lifetime. Spiritual Guardians have been known to you in your present lifetime and, if not, they are related to you and your family for being ancestors. (In that case, they may very well serve both functions). For example, I have had it occur on several occasions that a client feels a very strong connection to a great-grandparent whom they never met but for whom they feel a real bond. The connection may be made even more personal because the client shares a first or middle name with the deceased relative, or because the client has inherited a family heirloom that originally belonged to that ancestor.

In my experience, however, Guardians are most often loved ones in Spirit such as a parent or a grandparent, like the Turkish grandmother in the previous anecdote. Naturally, they have a vested interest in you and your well-being, and wish for you to make wise choices and smart decisions which include, of course, a healthy romantic partnership. Too often, people who are very desperate will pray to their deceased loved one with the expectation that the dearly departed will move mountains to make something good, great and positive happen. It's like praying every night for Mr. Right, the man of your dreams, to come galloping into your life on a white steed and sweep you off your feet. Romantic but not realistic.

Remember, your Guides and Guardians have a "hands off" policy, meaning they will not interfere or impose upon anyone's free will. But, they can drop hints, send you signs and inspire your dreams. So instead of saying, "Grandma, find me a nice guy before my next birthday!" try saying, "Grandma, I am open to whatever support and assistance you might offer for my greater good." It is always helpful to do this while holding that Guardian's picture or a small object that had belonged to them.

Another very intriguing component of the Guardian concept is that oftentimes a deceased parent, even a deceased ex-in-law or former spouse, who was addicted or abusive is better able to serve as a spiritual resource now that they have passed on. It occurs regularly in my psychic work that a parent who was absentee, selfish or emotionally inaccessible will come forward not only to apologize but to extend an olive branch in the form of an offer of assistance to serve as a Guardian and spiritual ally. In this way, and in their new and improved spiritual form, they desire to make up for lost time and for their earthly shortcomings. The caveat, of course, is for the recipient to be ready, willing and able to accept the apology, offer forgiveness and adjust how the relationship is now perceived. No one is obligated but when this occurs, it is a thing of great beauty and the peace that ensues only contributes to my clients' ability to release any bitterness they may harbor and elevate their mental-emotional, physical and spiritual energy—all of which contributes immeasurably to attracting the proper romantic partner.

The purpose of your Spirit Guide or Guardian(s) is to strengthen or enhance your own intuition, and to aid you in making decisions. The more you invest in this process of connectivity on a regular basis, the more you are likely to sense their presence, particularly when it comes to matters of the heart. You might imagine how helpful this may be when scanning online dating apps, accepting a blind or first date, or even discerning someone's truthfulness about their past relationships. This connection can be a useful tool, and you will wish to pay attention to note if your ordinary, everyday "gut instincts" are magnified for dialing up your spiritual team. Don't use them for finding romance exclusively; the most satisfying results will come when you least expect them and within the flow of the average day. Your Guide or Guardian will simply be available to encourage or refute any vibes you might be receiving. Stay connected and you'll be able to track how often they are correct for affirming your choices. That's a sure sign of working in tandem with them.

– Chapter 9 –

DREAM A LITTLE DREAM OF ME

Most people say they don't remember their dreams; but if you are invested in becoming more conscious and aware, you may also become increasingly aware of your dreams and how they might work to your advantage. Why do we dream to begin with? This is a question that has been explored and dissected for centuries. In my opinion, dreams serve several purposes. Dreams can simply be a time for a data dump, as in expunging any irrelevant fragments of emotional baggage you may still be carrying in addition to releasing what is no longer needed. In short, it may be an opportunity to de-stress and decompress subconsciously.

Similarly, your dreams may also be a vehicle by which you vent fears, frustrations and anxieties. Think of the childhood dreams you had in which you came to school and forgot your homework or were unprepared for a test. Other dreams of this nature would include those in which you have been feeling unworthy or inadequate and, in the dream, you are naked or in your underwear while everyone else is fully clothed. This kind of psychological expression of issues with which you've been grappling is commonplace in many people's dreams. If you're not addressing it in real life, it's only logical that it gets vented (and perhaps exaggerated) in dreams. It is one way the psychology of your mind purges itself of what has been disrupting your everyday thought processes.

Another function of your dreams may be to process, organize and prioritize information. If you're someone who is feeling spread too thin or is being pulled in many different directions by people demanding your attention, it may be challenging to compartmentalize your thoughts and create an agenda for meeting the needs of other as well as yourself. If you are one such individual, sleep is essential, and dreaming is mandatory. Your dreams are a form of meditation in which you are compelled to slow down and become a captive audience so to speak. If you are normally operating non-stop with all cylinders firing, your dreams may aid you to quell, calm and soothe your thoughts so that you are actually in a better position to sort things through while asleep. This is why you may awaken in the morning feeling as though you've been granted a fresh perspective or are feeling rejuvenated and prepared to face a new day.

If you are dealing with nightmares on a routine basis, the notion of going to bed and sleeping may be something you procrastinate because it has become so unpleasant. Frightening or unnerving dreams not only affect our psychology, they impair the quality of our ability to enjoy recuperative sleep, thus affecting us during waking hours; the mental and physical exhaustion certainly doesn't bode well toward raising the energy you project outwardly. If you are lonely and seeking love, it is possible that you are even sabotaging yourself in nightmares. You may be reliving an abusive relationship from the past or you may conjure a scenario in which you are feeling an attraction to someone that gets ignored or dismissed. Sometimes such dreams may be recurring, which is especially disconcerting as you can nearly count on them to repeat regularly like a bad TV rerun. What makes nightmares so destructive is how fatigued they make you feel after awakening, setting a tone for your attitude and mood and leaving you feeling defeated.

Conquering your nightmares is a possibility, however. Prior to going to sleep, take a few deep, cleansing breaths and set your intentions for what you expect of your sleep and your dreams. This may take some practice but be clear in stating that you will only allow yourself to be the recipient of dreams that are helpful, healing and humorous. If time allows, it's always good to soak in a nice hot bath before bed, scented with a comforting fragrance such as lavender. Water has a component of keen intelligence and will work with your body's energy to restore anything that is off-kilter. This is why we usually feel refreshed after a nice hot shower. Same goes for drinking water, as it will merge with the fluidity of your own body's tissues and organs to provide for your well-being.

If you are still troubled by unsettling dreams, another technique may be to envision yourself as an actor before going to sleep. (In dreams, you essentially are an actor, either as an observer or a participant, as none of it is real and all of it is pretend.) This is another instance of setting intentions with your mind prior to sleeping. What can occur, if you begin having a disturbing dream again, is that slowly but surely you begin to gain some control within the dream. It's something like being on a movie set and watching it all play out or going off-script and rewriting the scene you're in to better suit you— everyone's an actor and everything is simulated. Before long, you may find the upsetting dream dissipating altogether because you have disempowered any hold it may have over you. You'll notice the difference, as well, because while in the dream you'll be reclaiming advantage over orchestrating the events. In this manner, the nightmare isn't just happening to you, passively; instead, you are actively asserting control of the narrative and diffusing its ability to affect you negatively.

Dreams are also a two-way street by which your spiritual resources can connect with you. Just think of it; since birth, we've been conditioned to expect that, in dreams, anything is possible. In dreams, we are not only seeing vividly (and with our eyes closed!) but we may have superhuman abilities such as being able to fly, pass through solid objects, appear and disappear at will and even breathe underwater. Additionally, in dreams, you may have visions for what the future may bring, or you may be able to travel backwards in time to events of your childhood. It is possible that you may even gain glimpses of lifetimes prior to your own, which may inform your present-day likes, dislikes and phobias. All of these unique abilities may seem supernatural or paranormal to us but are natural and normal to our spiritual selves because all this and more is accessible to us in the hereafter. Such dreams are but a sampling of what may await us once we shed the dense armor that is our physical form.

In the previous chapter, Spirit Guides and Spirit Guardians were discussed. Your dreams can be a vehicle of communication for these spiritual energies, with your permission. You may have experienced something along these lines already, particularly if you were grieving a loss. Have you ever had a very lucid, vivid dream in which you were reunited with a deceased loved one? In the dream, you probably felt a sense of extreme elation and great joy for the opportunity to be in their presence once again. You may not even recall what was said or if anyone's mouth moved to speak, but you know powerful, loving emotion was exchanged. It's possible you awakened weepy and wanting more because it all felt so real. It may have also left you with the peace of serenity for knowing that your loved one is safe and well. Dreams such as this are called "visitations."

Visitations don't typical occur with any regularity. If they did, it would do more harm than good for becoming an unhealthy distraction to the point of preoccupation. Visitations are a "safe" way for the dearly departed to communicate because of the suspension of disbelief we understand is part and parcel of the dream experience. It is one way by which our loved ones can seek to comfort us and aid us in achieving some closure. Conversely, our guilt and shame can cause us to think we've had a visitation. For example, if you were unable to accommodate someone's final wishes or to coordinate the funeral service precisely according to their directions, you may be overcome with apprehension. However, any dream in which a deceased loved one is angry, doesn't respond to you, turns their back or walks away, is merely another form of psychological venting of anxiety while in the dream state. This is not the conduct of a soul that has transitioned to precisely the place it needs to be. In order to exist in the Heavenly Realm, no soul harbors ill will or resentments.

I have a friend that has seemingly mastered the concept of daydreaming or, as she terms it, manifesting. Our thoughts have extraordinary power, and if you ruminate enough on the worst-case scenario, you can worry something into being. Conversely, there is truth to the old adage, "If you believe it, you can achieve it." My friend does precisely this. When she finds that she needs added support and guidance, or requires answers to questions, she will daydream or go into a semi-trancelike state of being. With everything powered off and no distractions, she begins to visual what she would like to see happen in her life to propel things forward. She pictures it in her mind and visualizes it in detail. In this context, she also sets intentions for contributing her part to the process, such as anything she needs to be actively doing on her end. You can do this too, although if you have a short attention span, it may be useful to listen to a guided mediation in order to mentally get in "the zone." This is not a "once and done" process either; she keeps at it, breathing life into it and giving it agency on a regular basis until it manifests in real time.

Guess who she learned it from? When she was pressed into finding a new space to lease for her hair salon, she asked me to assist her in the manifestation process. Because she is a good and kind and decent human being, it was effortless for me to facilitate this on her behalf. What I envisioned for her was that the new space was actually in a house with red flowers in a stained-glass window. It wasn't a huge space but, because the building was old, it had a certain charm about it. Well, lo and behold, she found that the first floor of a house located just a mile from her was available for a business lease. She told me she knew it was the proper place as soon as she saw the stained-glass window in the bathroom with the red flowers woven into its design! I've actually manifested previous publications in this very same manner. Because the cover is what usually attracts someone to a book first, I start there by imagining its design including the title. I then flesh out the outline of various chapters in my mind, what territory each encompasses. If there are any pictures or photographs to be included, I'll start visualizing those as well, noting their placement within their respective chapters. There has not been a single instance for which the book that was visualized did not manifest to fruition.

Depending upon your self-discipline and commitment to this process (you have to remember to make time to do it), you may just be able to manifest a man! Again, this is a process that requires your attention and intention; and there are no promises or guarantees but you'll be no worse off for at least giving it a try. Don't allow urgency or desperation to cloud the process either, so quell and calm your mind prior to attempting this, such as in prayer or meditation beforehand. Do not become discouraged if you're expecting instantaneous results but be persistent in your practice once or twice a week.

Imagine creating the perfect partner from the ground up, as

if you were the one filling out his profile on a dating app. Consider his age, height and weight but also consider his ethnicity and background, his likes and dislikes (food, travel, music, pets), and whether he has been previously married or even has children of his own. Would he enjoy the same recreational interests as you or is it stimulating to explore all-new experiences with someone who is seasoned or knowledgeable about them? If you're reading this book, then you are probably more spiritually open to the metaphysical side of things; would he be as well, or would that be an educational journey of exposing him to your beliefs? Next begin to invest more effort into visualizing him. You know the age range, weight and height you'd consider but what about his facial features? It's likely not too realistic to imagine movie star good looks but what color are his eyes? (By the way, how many profile pics have you had to scroll through in which you can't even see his eyes because he's wearing dark sunglasses!) What about his hair? Does he still have hair? Does he resemble someone you have known previously? Is there a first name that you're getting? Keep at this process, as an artist gradually defines his subject's portrait, by adding more and more detail to it with each manifestation session. Then remain open to the potential to encounter someone that is very much in keeping with most, if not all, of what you've been projecting.

If you're still uncertain or lacking in confidence or self-discipline, another route to take would be to purposefully grant permission to sort all this out in your dreams. Just know that when you are asleep, you are at your most vulnerable, so ensure that you properly protect yourself with a prayer or a blessing prior to allowing permission for your higher self or a Higher Power, such as a Spirit Guide, to cooperate with you when dreaming. In your recitation, state the intention for what you'd like to see occur in your dreams. Be specific about it and express your desire to manifest a partner with whom you are a compatible friend and a loving ally, but also one that ticks all, or most, of the boxes you've defined. See what comes of it and keep a notepad and pen on your nightstand to jot down anything you can recollect upon awakening. See if you're not noticing patterns or themes emerging, or if they are any aspects that seem premonitory, such as a place or building you're supposed to encounter. Be aware of any déjà vu moments that may occur in real time, meaning there's a strong familiarity to the circumstances as if you've experienced it all before. It may be an indication that you're getting warmer, and closer, to Mr. Right in keeping with your dreams. This process is also a good option for problem solving whatever has been troubling you (that is, if the anxiety isn't causing you insomnia).

Again, before you attempt manifesting a man, relax and dispense with any sense of desperation as this may hinder the process by creating a mental blockage. To be relieved of the mental blockage, spend time listening to a guided mediation, spend time in prayer and contemplation, or simply listen to music that usually makes you feel good and puts you in a great mood. Then, have at it and give it a try! I have known of some success stories from any number of gals who were in the right frame of mind, felt confident in knowing who they were and what they wanted, and were able to attract him to them using this method. So, it can happen with some effort, time and patience.

– Chapter 10 –

TESTING THE CONNECTION

Let's say you've manifested your man or at least manifested a fella with whom you feel a comfortable kinship. How do you know if he's a long-term match or if the honeymoon period of current compatibility will endure? Well, beyond the obvious with regard to sharing a similar sense of humor, being passionate for liking the same activities or sexual compatibility, there are some ways in which you can "test the connection" so to speak. This will be especially helpful if you've felt an affinity with the content of this book or if you've been opening up by allowing your intuition to guide you. Learning to trust your gut is the single greatest obstacle to developing a sense of tranquil confidence in making good decisions and sound judgements; and that pertains to your love life as well. And when we're talking about a new relationship, therein lies the rub.

If you've been single for some time, it may be easy to fall in love very quickly or to think you're experiencing love when it's really infatuation. If that is the case, your judgement can be clouded. You may be leading with your heart (or your loins) instead of thinking with your head and, before you know it, old patterns of thought start re-emerging to sabotage the relationship. If you're sensing this may be true, reread the first several chapters of this book as a reminder to get grounded and collect your thoughts enough to get back on track. The excitement of being in a new relationship can be intoxicating and a lot of gals deliberately overlook or make excuses for what may be warning signs or red flags. This may lead to comprises that are regrettable.

So, what are some ways that you can apply your intuition to determine if you really are a match with your new mate? Here are some exercises that you can use behind the scenes in addition to some things you can try in his presence and in real time. As with anything that draws upon the spiritual and intuitive side of your personhood, be certain to always say a prayer or a blessing before enacting anything so that you are feeling safe and protected. Again, there is no specific language to be used, and examples of prayerful intentions have been provided in previous chapters. Ensure that you are alone and will have no disturbances to intrude upon your privacy. It may be helpful to listen to a meditation or some mood music to get yourself grounded and focused.

One of the easiest and simplest things you can do is to look at his photograph, a nice clear closeup of his face and in which he is not wearing sunglasses so you can see his eyes clearly. As odd as it may sound, make eye contact with him in the photograph, and stare into his eyes for a short time. Have with you a pad of paper and pen, and while looking at his picture repeat his first name three times. Then close your eyes for a moment or two and ask for the truth to flow through you effortlessly. When you open your eyes, start jotting down any impressions you receive in terms of thoughts or feelings or even images. Some of what you are jotting may be little drawings or doodles. When you feel as though this process has run its course, stop to assess your notes and see what you came up with. It will be interesting to see if the noted thoughts and feelings are in keeping with what you'd ordinarily be thinking and feeling, or if they contradict or conflict with such. If the latter, it may indicate the emergence of your inner, intuitive self trying to caution you. Pay attention to these sensations and keep comparing your notes with how the relationship is progressing.

A variation on this exercise is called automatic writing. During this process, you'll be actively engaging your Spirit Guide or other spiritual supports with whom you share a loving bond. In this instance, you'll actually be asking for these benevolent forces to take the lead. This may be a challenge if you are a take-charge or controlling kind of gal because it requires that you abdicate a lot of control to another energy other than your own. Think of the effect of blending or braiding your energy with that of those who adore you and want you to succeed. The preparation and setup is the same as before, only this time after you look at his photograph and repeat his name three times, close your eyes and press your pen to the paper. One of two things may happen. Either you'll not feel inclined to begin writing anything (and this may be because you're afraid of giving up control), or you may—slowly but surely—feel the pen start to move out from under you on its own accord. This initially may feel rather eerie but that sensation will pass as you grow accustomed to it. If this happens for you, try to release and go with the flow. Unlike the previous exercise, here you will keep your eyes closed the entire time. Don't feel compelled to be consciously and deliberately jotting things down, just allow the spiritual force to take the lead.

If you're feeling stuck because nothing's happening, stand up and shake your arms and move your body a bit. It may be that you're feeling too anxious or uptight, and that's creating a blockage. Try again but instead of waiting for the pen to move, start moving it yourself. Try drawing rows of spiraling circles or flowing lines just to get you loosened up. As you do this, gradually slow the process to a speed similar to how you would normally be writing things down. If you learned how to write in cursive, all the better as this will surely enhance the flow of energy as it translates to the paper. In fact, you may find in either case that what you've written is one continuous line.

Once you feel as though it's run its course, open your eyes and assess what you've done. At first glance, it may appear to be nothing more than a series of pleasantly pleasing swirls, dips and peaks. But try looking closer with a more objective eye. Are there any words that you are able to make out? It may be that you're not seeing anything relevant or as fluent as, say, reading the sentences in this book. It may be that there are random words that appear at various areas on the paper. When you pick them out, go over them in ink to reinforce the words. It may be a bit like connecting the dots; that is, on each page see if you can arrange the words in a manner that either forms a complete sentence or, if not, gives enough information to form a thought, such as if you're not seeing words but perhaps little icons or symbols that you are able to translate with meaning. For example, if you're seeing what looks like horseshoe shapes, do either of you have a connection to horses, a farm or stable? Or might this be an indicator of something for you both to explore as an activity together? If you're seeing what looks like a series of curving waves, might a shore vacation or other water-based activity be pending? Armed with this information, you can follow up with him to test his interest. If he bites and you both have an enjoyable time, there's all the confirmation you'll need to validate the automatic writing process!

With patience and practice, you may find this a valuable tool that grants you insight and perspective, not only into how the relationship is progressing but also for ideas and suggestions to enrich the bond you both share with one another. Eventually, you'll be able to ask questions in this manner and feel better able to trust that you will receive answers, though you may not always like what you receive. And that's a caveat to working in collaboration with such a wise and powerful force: Spirit doesn't tell us what we want to hear, Spirit tells us what we need to hear. Because you have free will, you can choose to deny or ignore what's conflicting with your own ego. That's not going to change things, it just means it may take longer for you to realize the truth of what Spirit is trying to tell you. After all, it's for the greater good of your highest order.

Another technique to try is to hold a small personal object

belonging to your new boyfriend, preferably something metal such as a ring, necklace, belt buckle, keys or watch. Why metal? Because the metal retains and stores the energy of the person with whom it has come in contact most. As such, it is the keeper of a lot of information about its user that your intuitive self may tap into. Gaining permission to use a personal object belonging to him may be tricky without arousing his suspicions unless you can temporarily "borrow" it and quickly replace it unnoticed. As with the previous exercises, you'll also want to be certain that you get yourself alone and free from all distractions and disturbances once you obtain said object.

Also as before, ensure that you say a prayer or a blessing before attempting to do anything so that you feel properly protected and free from any undue influences that may cloud your abilities of perception. Again, if you need to listen to a guided meditation or mood music feel free to do so as it can only enhance the experience. You may wish to have pen and paper handy to jot down anything you want to remember. Sit with the metal object in your hand and wait to see if you start receiving any impressions from it. This process actually has a name; it's called psychometry, which is the intuitive and energetic gathering of information connected to objects. You may actually feel the metal object quickly heat up in your hand as its energy connects, and transfers, to your own energy.

What is likely to be most telling is how the object makes you feel as soon as you are holding it. Does its presence in your hand feel light or heavy? Does it call to mind any particular emotions? It is pleasant to hold the object, or does it make you feel anxious? Next, see if you receive any impressions of colors from the object. You might even "see" such colors mentally in your mind's eye. Bright or pastel colors would obviously connote happiness and playfulness. Red, gray, black or muddy brown would possibly associate with anger issues, dependency or addiction, or other mental-emotional concerns of well-being. Trust your gut instinct on this, even if it is disappointingly opposed to everything you want to believe about the relationship. The energy the metal object gives off is unbiased and doesn't take sides, it simply is what it is.

Supposing these exercises do contradict what your heart is making you believe? It doesn't mean that he's a bad person or that you should overreact by terminating the relationship immediately. Interpret these impressions as you would a road sign, cautioning you about slippery curves ahead. In other words, it's a communication to pay careful attention and proceed with caution. Don't rush into anything, such as an engagement or moving in together if you are consistently receiving these conflicting messages. Also, as the relationship grows and improves, you may find the results of these exercises shifting more positively and in reflection of the direction in which things are heading. And that's encouraging, if so. If there is cause for any concern, it will reveal itself before long and you won't need to be a psychic to see it coming. One slip-up may be forgivable as someone having an "off" day, but two or more indicate a behavioral pattern that should inform you moving forward.

Let's say things are rolling along just great and you are feeling a wonderful and affirming connection to your new fella. The future's looking bright and you have been fantasizing about what your future together may look like a year or more down the road. Such a strong and positive connection would surely yield a greater potential for psychic symbiosis or what is scientifically referred to as entrainment. Entrainment is what occurs biologically when we naturally fall into a synchronized motion, such as walking and breathing at the same time and rate. Entrainment may also pertain to what occurs when the rhythm of our heart and our brain waves align within ourselves and from one to another. Its unified pulse strengthens the bond and solidifies the connection between hearts and minds with those we love.

If you experience this sensation with him, try seeing how adept he is at picking up on your unspoken communication. I'm not talking about dropping hints about something you want or need in the hopes that he will put two-and-two together. This is about seeing if you are able to reach him on a whole other plane of thought without using words. You may have already experienced something very much like this already. It's called mother's intuition. It's an internal knowingness that you are needed in that very same moment; you don't know how you know, but you know! If you have children, there's probably been occasions when you felt an urging to go to your child and check on them, especially as an infant or toddler. If they are older, you may have felt compelled to call or text them and, sure enough, they were thinking of you or needing you in that exact moment. That sensation is entrainment between you and your child. You don't even have to be a mother to experience it. Many pet owners will tell you that their animal companions are members of the family. You may have enjoyed entrainment with your pet irrefutably, which makes it all the more powerful because while they don't speak, they communicate in many ways including psychically through telepathy, as was discussed in the chapter on pets.

An exercise you can try with your human companion is that of sending a thought or feeling to see if he is able to receive it. That might be a strong indicator for the fortitude of your bond in the relationship at this particular point in time. You can be in separate rooms or many miles apart, the distance makes no difference. Make whatever preparations you need, as before, in terms of getting in "the zone." Set the intention that you wish him to reach out and contact you. If you are in the same location, it could mean he calls out to you or comes to where you are; if you are apart from one another, then the expectation would be that he calls or texts you.

Next, focus on everything you enjoy and adore about him, from his physical attributes to his quirks to his sense of humor to the way he expresses romance. Spend a good five minutes or so in thought, bringing to mind the very best of what attracts you to him. Enjoy the sensation that comes over you in keeping with these thoughts—that's the entrainment aligning. You may even feel a shivery tingling or goosepimple sensation on your skin in addition to pleasant, loving thoughts. When you complete this process, give it another ten to fifteen minutes for him to "receive" what you've "sent." The rapidity with which he responds could be an indicator of how closely attuned you are to one another. But for goodness sakes, don't panic if he doesn't get back to you immediately, if at all. It's not a scientific experiment; it's just for fun so don't lose sleep over it. Also to be considered is that the majority of men are simply not intuitive in nature, they tend to be more literal and concrete for needing tangibles. What you're attempting may simply be too esoteric for him, but that doesn't make him a bad person or an ill-fitted match.

For many couples, an intuitive connection is something that is cultivated as the relationship progresses and endures, and that takes time, even years. So don't be discouraged but do keep trying to see if he eventually gets best out of three attempts, or one really good "hit" that speaks to being more than coincidence. The lack of entrainment doesn't mean the train has derailed. It just means that where you fella is concerned, you have to, lovingly, hit him over the head with a cement block to say what you mean and mean what you say. That is until the attunement gets aligned and flows with less effort.

If things are getting serious between the two of you, you'll probably be introduced to his family at some future point. His relationship (or lack thereof) with his surviving parents or siblings can be very telling in terms of emotional stability and commitment to his family unit. Estrangement or indifference may speak volumes about them, him or both parties. This could extend to whether he is potentially good father material if you are still of childbearing age and desire to be a mother. If he didn't have a father or a positive male role model, he may be unequipped to parent a child for lacking the emotional intelligence to do so. On the other hand, if he had a difficult mother or an abusive father, he may be of the personality type to put effort into making certain he doesn't perpetuate the cycle but, instead, breaks it.

In advance of meeting his family, you'll naturally want to know something about them and see photos of them as well. But if you are able, try curbing your desire to have him fill you in, in favor of just requesting their photos. Like most people in today's world, the photos will probably be digital and not hard copy. If they are hard copy, ask to borrow them; if digital, ask him to send them to you. As with all the prior exercises, prepare yourself and be in a quiet, distraction-free space in which you can focus on particular people in the photos. If his parents are still living, you may wish to start there. Jot down some notes, whatever comes to mind, for any first impressions you receive, just from looking at them. Do this for any siblings or extended family to whom you expect to be introduced.

When you're able to, debrief with him. You can frame it with him in the context of you testing your intuition to see how close you get to "guessing" their personality; or you could more casually ask leading questions from memory. You might wonder something like, "Was your mother unhappy?" You may feel validated if he tells you that his mother has long been depressed. Or you might suggest, "Your dad looks like an all-around good guy," to which he may respond, "Yeah, he's great. He's everybody's friend." This intuitive information will inform how best to navigate making a good first impression on the family, as well as who could be your champion or who to interact with as little as possible to keep the peace.

One last word before this chapter wraps. It is entirely possible that any man you begin seeing has children in any age range. You will obviously want to like them as much as you will desire to be liked. Ingratiating yourself to them will also be a process. Depending upon whether the split between their parents was acrimonious or amicable, they could be leery of you, the new woman in their father's life. One of the most important ways to connect with his children is to identify their most passionate of interests and then ask them to show or teach you all about it. This scenario has all the potential to set a precedent for an emotionally satisfying and unifying experience. Nothing makes a child feel more important or validated than to feel as though they have something of value to offer, especially to an eager adult.

Where there is skepticism or resentment toward you, try to find some common ground. After all, you were once their age too. In your meditation time, try focusing on recollecting what it was like to be eleven, sixteen, twenty and so on. What were your worries or concerns? What brought you joy? And so maybe the next time you interact with his children, instead of asking lots of questions of them you could begin by telling them stories of what you recall when you were the same age. I actually counseled a client about this very thing not long ago. She was dating a man who was a widower and had a teenage daughter. The daughter seemed completely disinterested in my client and yet was fiercely protective of her dad. Despite numerous attempts, my client was unable to establish any sort of connection with this girl, which was frustrating to her.

But what was being overlooked, however, was the obvious. Not only did this teenage girl lose her mother, my client had also lost her mother at a young age as well. I suggested to my client that that was the place to begin. That, at the next opportune moment, she should tell this girl that she understands how she feels and to share her story about how she survived it and was able to overcome the worst of the grief. During this conversation, the Spirit of my client's mother came forward and directed my client to gift to the girl a piece of the deceased mother's jewelry to reinforce this show of goodwill. As far as I know, this worked, and the token gift resonated as much more than a gift but a peace offering from which a new relationship could blossom.

Chapter 11

CHILDREN

If you've reached the point of talking about having a baby with your male companion, then things have progressed to the point of being serious for an extended commitment. By now you've determined that he's the one you envision spending the rest of your life with, and you both desire to have a child together. It's a big step but one that can also be guided spiritually in keeping with all preceding information you've been learning in this book.

In the manner of manifesting the ideal mate, you can do this for your baby as well. Believe it or not, you can make an effort to connect to the soul of your future baby before he or she is born! That's right, there's a precious little soul looking down on you and waiting for the opportune moment to make its presence known to you. I have interviewed any number of children who informed me that they deliberately chose their parents prior to being born. One little boy told me he clearly remembered being in Heaven before he came down to Earth. He said he was offered a choice before incarnating, that it was a decision between his new parents and a Japanese couple. He chose his birth parents because he thought learning to read, write and speak in Japanese would be too hard!

To enact the process of manifesting your baby, start as you previously have by getting yourself alone in a quiet space free from all distractions and interruptions. The relationship you establish with the unborn baby's soul is no different from a relationship you might have with any Higher Power with which you commune and in which you place your trust. You'll benefit from the relationship based on what you project and invest in it. In this meditation time, begin by communicating to the soul, in your thoughts, that you would be honored to be its mother, and you are welcoming and ready to receive it. It will be a partnership process that begins before conception and will endure for the duration of the pregnancy and through the lifespan of your child. Begin by seeing if you can sense the soul. Is it male or female? Do you feel any particular emotions during these intimate bonding moments? Is there a feeling that the desire to unite with one another is mutual? These are things to be considering.

One mother got very specific during this process, sensing not one but two souls. She decided they were twin girls that wished to be born together. She even noted that each had different-color eyes, one blue and one hazel. Well, she got her wish when she gave birth to twin girls with exactly those eye colors. The one with blue eyes she named Violet, and the other was named Hazel! Another client recently told me how strongly connected she's always been to her daughter and when she showed me a picture of her daughter, I could see why. Her daughter was striking in appearance with long blonde hair, beautiful skin and sparkling blue eyes—a truly lovely young woman. But more than her physical attractiveness, I immediately intuited something else about the daughter. "Your daughter is very psychic," I said. "Yes," my client told me, "I've always known that." As we were talking, I was feeling that my client and her daughter shared a stronger bond, like they had known one another before but not in a past life. My client explained that she had had a twin who perished in a house fire when both girls were three years old. My client somehow managed to stumble towards the front door and, falling against it, pushed it open before she collapsed, thus allowing in the fresh air she needed to survive. "I believe my daughter is my sister, returned to me," she said, and I had to agree.

So, you see, the bond between you and the soul of your future baby may not be as foreign and unusual as you may think. You may already have had a history with it, whether in this lifetime or in a past life. Like a flock of sheep, we never stray far from the fold. What this means is that, in my experience, souls tend to remain grouped together over successive lifetimes that manifest in family units. They do this in order to cycle through a variety of life lessons and experiences within that specific grouping. Now, that doesn't mean that one soul always takes the role of mother, another always as father, and so on. That would get monotonous! No, the family dynamic gets switched out as we assume different roles. For example, you could have been your current mother's father and she your son in a previous lifetime! As crazy as it sounds, I am confident that it will all make perfect sense when we eventually get to where we're going. So much has been orchestrated in advance, but not all is necessarily set in stone.

One long-time client was wavering in her indecision for having a second child. When she was newly married, I not only predicted that she was intended to be a mother, I foresaw that first child would be a little girl. When I told her this, she looked at me like I was nuts! Having a baby was the furthest thing from her mind. In fact, she told me very plainly she did not want to be a mother. Well, guess what happened! She not only had the baby girl, but she also discovered that she loves being a mother to her. She's been coming to me for a number of years now and for a period of about five years afterwards, I kept telling her I was sensing a male soul that wanted to be her son. I even gave her the name: Christopher. She told me how odd that was because she and her husband had been fantasizing what they would name a future son, and they decided on Kit, which is a nickname for Christopher!

From then on, she began connecting to Kit's soul, in the manner I've described here, talking with him in quiet, pensive times. But when it came to more actively being a mother a second time, and trying to conceive, her position had been, "If it happens, it happens." In other words, lacking was real desire and motivating intention. Each year she came to me, and each year the little Christopher soul came through, expressing his wish to be born to her. He even said he might be born with Down syndrome but, if he were, there could be no better family than my client's in which to be born because they had all the love and support that he required. Interestingly, my client was not fazed or alarmed by this news, and concurred that Down syndrome was nothing she and her husband couldn't handle. This went on for a good five years, as I said, until during our most recent session he failed to come through. Puzzled, I tried to connect but there was just nothing, emptiness. The impression I got was that the window of opportunity had closed, and after many years of trying, Christopher had moved on. It was a melancholy feeling but the decision was never mine to make.

In another unique instance, I was conducting a psychic reading with a client, and I also told her that she was supposed to have a baby. She was taken aback! She told me she had a twenty-one-year-old son and a seven-year-old daughter. "I'm done!" she said emphatically. I explained that having another child could look a lot of different ways, even to temporarily caring for someone else's child but she was adamant. "Well, I'm seeing a little boy," I countered. "Huh, hmmm…" she replied. Neither one of us thought anything of it and we continued the session. Curiously enough, she reached out to me a couple weeks later. She had recorded her reading with me and had only just listened back to it. She couldn't believe what she heard and sent me the sound bite from the recording. At the point during which I'm telling her she's to have a baby and that it could be a son, there's a child's voice that audibly says, "I'm ready for you." Unbelievable! We were the only two people in the building at the time and there's no logical explanation for the voice to have turned up on the recording and in that moment, as if to give what I was saying certain emphasis. I did ask my client if she had reconsidered and she told me she had asked her husband about it, and he said that he had kind of been thinking about the possibility of having another child. I never did find out if they did, but I can confidently say that a little soul was letting them know he was ready and willing!

Speaking of little souls, I regularly encounter female clients who carry with them guilt and shame for having terminated a pregnancy in their youth. As was discussed earlier in this book, from a spiritual perspective, there is no right or wrong under these circumstances. But, most amazingly, what I have been shown during my psychic sessions with them is that—in hindsight—the pregnancy would have happened at an inopportune time and with the wrong person. So, in a sense, everyone evaded a regrettable situation for that brief moment in time including both partners, their respective families and also the soul of what would have been the child who would have been born into a conflicted and uncertain future.

Just as amazing is that I am also shown that the soul of what was the terminated pregnancy returns to its Heavenly home and waits. Oftentimes, as I am channeling a client's deceased relative, be it a mother or grandparent, they come through holding the soul energy of an infant to come. They show me this by forming a cradle with their arms and gently rocking the baby's energy. But they also indicate that this is an infant soul that will be making a renewed effort to return to the family, in reference to the pregnancy that was previously terminated. If my client is still of childbearing age, then the soul's return marks its potential for a homecoming with its original mother. If my client already has adult children, then it is a reference to the soul returning to the family fold as a grandchild, believe it or not. I always tell each client that she will know for certain once she holds the newborn infant in her arms for the first time and gazes upon him or her; and I have had clients validate this meaningful connection for me. It's as though the soul knows its purpose is to somehow, someway, be in each client's life even if it has to wait until it can be a grandchild.

On a regular basis I sit across from any number of young women of childbearing age who are desperate to get pregnant but, for the life of them, simply cannot conceive. If you've ever found yourself in this situation, you may well be able to sympathize with the exhaustion and frustration of repeated efforts and attempts that simply do not bear fruit. When faced with a client such as this, my first inclination is to do a full body scan to see if I can identify any physical reason why she has been unable to conceive. This is a very quick and easy process and requires nothing from my client other than to simply sit still for a few moments. I start at the top of her head and work my way downwards. As I make my way to her female organs, nearly one hundred percent of the time I see them depicted almost in a cartoon fashion. The fallopian tubes become arms and hands that clap and coax, as if to say, "We are ready! C'mon bring it, let's do this!" Everything else looks healthy and robust and, to my eyes, there's absolutely no reason why my client shouldn't be able to get pregnant, and they usually confirm this is in keeping with their doctors' assessment as well.

Seeing that everything is just fine, female organ-wise, I reroute back to her head and hone my focus there. Also, nearly one hundred percent of the time, this is where I find the blockage. You see, it is almost always not a physical health concern but a mental health concern. For whatever reason, too many young women are applying so much pressure and anxiety to conceiving a pregnancy—which may include outside pressures being imposed upon them—that they have created a mental blockage which sabotages the entire process. Can you believe our minds have that kind of power as to veto and override bodily functions? But time and time again this is what I see.

The most obvious solution is to encourage each client in such a predicament to relax but that may be easier said than done. What I have found most helpful is for both my client and her mate to get out of town, to go away on a mini vacation beyond the environment that has incited the angst and frustration. If plans are made to enhance the long weekend or overnight stay in ways that are romantic, all the better. The goal is to not only relax but to rekindle the romance, to rediscover one another and to restore the spark of sexual chemistry that attracted both parties to one another in the first place. This can occur by revisiting a specific place that holds good memories from the past or by doing something especially romantic such as a quiet dinner out or participating in an activity of interest to both. Many times, I have had young women come back to me to report having done this and, as things got amorous, they humorously sensed in the spark of conception, "That just took!" And, indeed, it most often does.

Finally, it's entirely possible that the man you meet already has children or perhaps you do, yourself. This situation obviously brings with it a whole new dynamic as various personalities effort to blend and braid and coalesce in a Brady Bunch kind of relationship. More often than not, this is a process and one that may take a long time to gel depending upon the underlying circumstances that contributed to each partner now being single. There may, in fact, be animosity toward you or your partner on the part of one or more of his children. In all fairness, the source of such conflicted emotions may not be entirely authentic in motive.

In my psychic readings, I have had it happen on many occasions that a deceased father comes through in Spirit who was long considered by his children to have been a cheater and a deadbeat. He may have left the family or traveled a lot for business or had one or more affairs on the side. What these men come through to communicate is that they were not bad people, they just made bad choices. They also tell us that not everything their children were told about them was entirely true. And indeed, my clients will often confess that, years later, they learned to a great extent that their mother and other family members falsely portrayed their fathers as unreliable, unavailable and spiteful when, in fact, the truth lies somewhere in between. These men aren't trying to skirt the issues and avoid accountability, they only wish to present their side of the story by telling me they're not the villain. Oftentimes, they suffered in silence, tolerating the abusive accusations without defending themselves for not wanting to exacerbate an already stressful situation. They also show me that their wives weaponized sex by withholding it as a punishment. They'll cop to having been a man with a male sex drive and, feeling the urge, crawled into bed only to have their wives roll over and turn their back to them. As one father in Spirit said, "What's a fella to do?" They also indicate that, not taking their penis with them where they are now, they have a different perspective absent that sex drive. My point in sharing all this is to be conscious and aware going into a new relationship, in which one or both parties already has children, that feelings and opinions may well be colored by half-truths or blatant lies.

Over the years, I've channeled hundreds of such deceased fathers who were unfaithful over the course of their marriage, either because of disharmony at home, because of an intense libido, or because their wives became averse to sexual intimacy. I'm not judging or making excuses, but it is what it is. One Sunday afternoon, I had a deceased father come through who remained married to my client's mother for decades even though he had numerous affairs. But he offered an explanation I had never heard before in my years as a professional medium. He praised his wife (also now in Spirit) and spoke of how lovely, poised and dignified she was, and said she was too much of a lady for him to degrade her by satisfying his frequent, impulsive sexual needs. And so, he preserved her dignity and gratified his needs elsewhere in superficial encounters that had nothing to do with the respect he had for his wife, though some would disagree. (I've come to understand that among Italian Catholic males this rationale is called the Madonna Effect.) My job is to be an impartial third party and not get emotionally involved, but I have to admit that his confession was so genuine that I teared up. My client understood completely her father's position and closed our session by offering her forgiveness—a reminder to grant some grace for our very real human flaws and frailties.

Also know that, from a spiritual perspective, there is no "half" or "step" or "adopted" anything. What this means is that, in the grand scheme of how the Universe ultimately operates, we end up with who we are intended to be with, regardless of whether or not those who raise us are blood relations or biological family. It makes no difference if there is diversity in ethnicity, heritage or cultural background. In each lifetime, there are soul lessons to be learned in order for us to grow and evolve from the culmination of experiences that get imprinted and recorded upon the soul's essence. It's fascinating how some siblings, born to the same biological parents, drift apart or become estranged for having little to no emotional connection, while some families comprised of adopted or foster children are every bit as bonded, if not more so, than biologically related siblings. Regardless, attempting to create unity in a blended situation brings its own challenges and, as noted, requires time and patience while everyone gets acclimated and adjusted. But maybe, just maybe, being dad's new girlfriend or even the eventual stepmother is the soul opportunity you never knew you needed.

– Chapter 12 –

GROWING TOGETHER, GROWING APART

Let's say you've employed all the techniques and strategies you've read about in this book, and you have finally manifested a connection with a man with whom you can begin to envision a long-term relationship. It's about time, right! And as much as it's been a long time in coming, it's important to remember not to relapse into old patterns of thought that could threaten to sabotage the relationship because you are too anxious, needy or clingy. It's important to keep perspective and recognize that your current man is not your ex—because that was then and this is now. You've elevated your energy and are emitting a far healthier frequency that has attracted to you a compatible mate that is not your ex, because he is also of a higher-vibration frequency. So, congratulations and enjoy being in the moment as it unfolds.

If you're fortunate, among the things that bond you both are mutual passions and special interests, such as hobbies. In my psychic work, it's interesting to see how so much of what couples enjoy doing together has its roots in past lifetime identities. For example, the antique car enthusiasts who spend their weekends and free time reconditioning and restoring old cars before driving them to collectors' gatherings. I have seen that the particular period of time for which they each most relate to is reflected in the make, model and year of their favorite cars. The couples who enjoy traveling to various music concerts and festivals may also have been united in a similar way specific to the eras in which their music was at its peak of popularity. This may even extend to where you both decide to vacation, as it may also recall familiarity with the culture and locales in which your previous lifetimes were set. It's intriguing to consider how little of what we experience is by random coincidence.

In one situation, a client of mine, who was a young woman in her early thirties, felt drawn to attend World War II collectors' shows in which people attended in vintage 1940s-era clothing and uniforms. She always felt so comfortable in her various costumes because not only did the clothing suit her well, it seemed to transport her to another time and this translated to her posture, vocabulary and values. She became friendly with an attractive gentleman dressed in army fatigues who was about eighteen years older than she. Between them there was not only a mutual passion for the 1940s and World War II, there was a nearly palpable sexual chemistry and they became a steady couple, courting as people did in an era before either one was ever born.

In my psychic session with her, I saw that this client and her newfound beau definitely shared a previous lifetime together, but then, she had actually been the toddler daughter of her boyfriend who had been her father at the time! He enlisted in the army but, sadly, did not return home for being missing in action. Their connection not only rekindled the closeness of the relationship, it was an effort to compensate for time lost due to losing her father at such a very young age. And before any reader feels uncomfortable about this kind of situation, please know that any incestuous overtones have been erased in this lifetime; the souls are only focused on reuniting in their new identities in order to reestablish a continuation of the relationship.

Any number of my clients who have been married for longer than a decade often feel somewhat disconnected from their husband, as if the honeymoon period has worn thin and things are in a holding pattern. As a practicing psychic, I can provide intuitive guidance and insight into what the future may hold, but that does not make me a relationship expert or a marriage counselor. In my opinion, it is inappropriate to consult a psychic about the status of your marriage, especially where unrealistic suspicions arise such as when clients ask me, "Is my husband cheating on me?" If you're to the point of asking that question, then you are past due for getting professional support. And this is precisely what I tell each of my clients, that a psychic is not a substitute for marriage counseling and therapy. What I will tell them is the decision to remain in a marriage with which they are dissatisfied and unhappy is entirely up to them, but I will do my best to offer some guidance to project where things may be heading.

It is, perhaps, natural for a woman who has previously only known abusive or disillusioning relationships to be anxious about whether or not the current relationship will turn out similarly. But that anxiety is a destructive function of ego that can lead to paranoia and preoccupation, and that can cause the dissolution of a marriage every bit as much as an unfaithful spouse. I've seen it, from the smothering, constant need for reassurances of his love, to the suspicious grilling for accountability of his whereabouts, to the constant checking of his text messages and website search history. In such situations, trust has clearly eroded, and the relationship is in trouble. If you are prone to these tendencies, please revisit the technique discussed earlier in this book for blocking and halting disruptive patterns of thought that serve no purpose other than to cause you to self-deprecate. You and your male companion will both be thankful that you have broken a cycle of obsessive clinginess.

Along these lines of thought, in order for both parties to feel free from suffocating on too much togetherness, each of you needs time apart from one another to do your own thing. In my line of work, this usually pertains to a woman coming into her own spiritually, awakening her consciousness and opening up to unlimited possibilities—not just about the Universe but about herself. This most often tends to be women in their late-thirties to early-forties who are coming to terms with reconciling a traditional religious upbringing with a growing sense of personal spirituality. In a number of instances, these gals also wish to further explore or pursue the potential to become involved in the metaphysical and holistic wellness community on a vocational basis.

I am never one to discourage these pursuits, but the caution is several-fold. First, do your homework and understand what knowledge needs to be gleaned in order to be properly accredited or certified in each respective, chosen field. Second, and depending upon exactly what such pursuits may entail, be mindful of when, where and with whom you discuss what may be some pretty far out, even paranormal, concepts. It is not universally embraced, and it would not be ethically advised to attempt to sway or even indoctrinate anyone who is not ready and willing to receive the information, despite your obvious enthusiasm. And third, your partner isn't obligated to be on board and on the same page as you, so don't try forcing the issue without expecting resistance. If exploring your spirituality in consideration of offering some professional service is a new idea for you, it's even newer for your male companion. You have evidently been investing some time and thought into your evolution, and it is calling (or pulling!) you in a different direction; and that's not what your partner signed up for when you and he first met.

In my opinion, it is unreasonable to expect him to actively participate in something he doesn't understand or struggles to accept given his own background and perhaps conflicted emotions about religion, spirituality and things that are not readily and rationally explained. Now, it's one thing if he is outright vocal and dismissive or even if he forbids you to involve yourself in such pursuits. That's cause for either putting a pause on the relationship or offering to educate him on whatever it is you are exploring. But if he is perfectly fine with you going off to do your own thing and kisses you goodbye with a "Have fun!" and "So long," let it be. He's doing the best he knows how to in the moment. He doesn't have to keep pace with your rate of evolution if he's not yet personally attained a similar degree of understanding. No one is to blame. So, please, do have fun but leave it at the door when you get home...unless he asks!

If you feel as though you're sprouting off in a different direction while he's remaining static and content with the "same old, same old," there may be nothing more gratifying than to have him begin to express his curiosity for where you've been and what you've been doing. This demonstrates his investment in the relationship as well as a budding yearn to be educated by you, his partner in love. When this happens, be grateful but also be mindful of not inundating him with too much information. Gently feed it to him piecemeal so he won't be overwhelmed or, worse yet, turned off because it sounds so foreign to his sensibilities. Follow his lead and only share as much information as he seems comfortable digesting.

One of the great strategies that Spirit has guided me to inform my female clients in this type of situation is to be open to the possibility of involving your man in whatever it is that you are exploring. I'm not talking about suggesting he enroll and join you in a class or a program; I'm talking about asking him to contribute some form of his expertise to your vision and growth process, even if temporarily. It's not disingenuous if you are sincere about it, and it will help him feel both valued and no longer left out, if he has been feeling a bit neglected.

For example, one of my clients felt she was ready to launch her own small business, and though she had the passion and drive, she lacked the financial smarts to navigate the logistics of organizing things properly. What was eluding her, however, was not being able to see the forest for the trees; her own husband was an accountant and would have the basic understanding of what would need to be in place and, if he didn't, he was at least in a position to connect her to associates of his that could. Problem solved: she received the necessary supports from someone whom she loved and who was better equipped to contribute something he understood well (and which she did not) as opposed to being baffled, or even alienated, by her continued pursuits that did not involve him. If you find yourself in a similar situation, approach your male partner and ask him for help and assistance. It may be just the thing to make him feel that he is being supportive and yet still allowing you autonomy to do your thing.

As you well know, not all relationships are smooth sailing all the time and, if they are, something must be amiss. Job stress, problems with your children or pets, and financial worries can stir the pot to fray nerves and fan tempers. A lot of us experience such stressors on a daily basis to the extent that these intrusions are nuisances that can usually be overcome. But on occasion, something truly tragic and catastrophic can occur that is devastating. As you might imagine, in my work as a psychic medium, I am approached by clients who have, indeed, suffered horrific losses. Such losses are compounded by their sudden unexpectedness such as a loved one perishing in an automobile accident or the teenage son who died as the result of a drug overdose. These experiences are life-altering and, where romantic partnerships are concerned, such situations often strain the commitment.

As was discussed previously when couples were struggling to conceive, please also know that when tragedies occur, they are not without purpose. That may sound insensitive to those of you still raw and stinging from a recent, tragic loss. It is a form of grace that the passage of time can grant us the perspective of hindsight. When I am confronted by a situation like this that unfolds before me in a psychic session, one of the things I ask my clients is, "What have you learned?" or "Has this experience taught you anything?" I have witnessed the extraordinary grace of many women who have gained in wisdom and enabled their voice to articulate exactly what they have gained as a result of surviving such a tragedy.

Perhaps nothing is more difficult than the sudden loss of a child, whether it is a suicide, a murder or an accident. Many marriages crumble under the stress of guilt, shame or accusations of blame. But I have seen that—in the grand scheme of the Universe—the loss always provides an opportunity. There is hope for reunification where things were contentious and there is a chance to strengthen bonds of solidarity already firmly entrenched. I have had a number of deceased kids and teens in Spirit explain this to me (sometimes with good humor and in their own style of slang). It may not make sense to those loved ones left behind, but I receive assurances that when we get to their plane of existence one day, it will all make perfect sense that things happened the way that they did.

That's a small comfort to the grieving parents trying to cope with the here and now. But I have seen ex-wives and ex-husbands rally around one another, and become far more caring, civil, patient and compassionate with one another than they ever would have been if the loss had not occurred. I have had children in Spirit implore that their divorced mothers reach out to their fathers because the fathers are grappling so hard but holding it all inside, such that they are like an emotional ticking time bomb ready to explode. Please know that this extends to the status of your relationship when you suffer a tragic blow; it will likely either explode, implode, strengthen in its resolve or a combination of all three at different stages of the recovery process.

A number of my female clients tell me they are bored in their long-term relationship, whether it is a partnership or a marriage. They feel a lack of excitement and stimulation as life has fallen into a predictable pattern. All relationships ebb and flow and stagnate from time to time; and, so, my first reaction is to tell them that boring is good, boring is great, especially given the preceding discussion about the tragic turn things may take at any given moment. No one is guaranteed another moment, and we should be grateful for our health, safety and welfare and that of our loved ones on a daily basis. The next reaction is to ask what part of that boredom is the responsibility of my client. The victim routine doesn't work with me because, over the course of my life, I have chosen to disavow being a victim even though I could very easily have chosen that path given my history of having been verbally abused and physically harassed. Nor does an attitude of entitlement sway me. If your relationship has lost its luster, what are you doing to restore it? What efforts have you invested in shaping it to be more of what you desire it to be? If you believe in your heart that you have done all you can and you still feel stagnated, then there are some things to be considering.

As you well know, either because you, yourself, are divorced or separated, or because your parents divorced or separated, people change over time. The person you fell in love with may not be the same person that causes you to now question that love. Not every relationship or marriage is intended to be forever and that's okay! Not only do people change as they grow and mature and find their voice (or become emboldened to better advocate for themselves), they also grow apart. And as you may have already experienced, people fall out of love with one another. It doesn't mean the relationship has to end in acrimony, it may simply be that it has run its course, and it is time for both parties to move on.

During psychic sessions I have sat across from any number of women who are presently married but co-existing under the same roof with a man to whom they feel obligated despite a lack of reciprocity. That they decide to stay is their choice. One client has been dreadfully unhappy for many years in her marriage, but she chooses to remain because she doesn't wish to upset the balance of the household where her children are concerned. Is she being shortsighted by denying herself happiness or is she making a noble sacrifice? Life is all about making a series of choices. It really is about what you make it to be. If you choose to stay, you obviously can't rely upon your mate to provide you with happiness; that you'll have to find elsewhere with friends or through volunteering or by working. If you choose to leave, it may be like the mother bird that nudges its babies to take wing and leave the nest. The outcome may have a life-changing effect on you and be a wake-up call to the man you leave behind.

– Chapter 13 –

LOVE AFTER DEATH

A couple years ago, I was conducting a psychic session with a young woman when a female presence in Spirit came through identifying herself as having a "J" name and showing me the little pink ribbon that represents breast cancer awareness. My client gasped—it was Joanne, a friend of her mother's, who had passed with breast cancer leaving behind her husband of many years. As so often occurs, because it was my client that was sitting with me, and not her mother or Joanne's husband, Joanne took advantage of the opportunity to be heard as there was no telling when, or even if, there would be another chance to do so. My client was more than gracious in granting Joanne as much time as she needed, even though her coming through was completely unexpected.

Joanne wanted to express her love to all who knew her and were still here in physical form. She then showed me Sonny and Cher, a musical-comedy team popular in my youth during the

1960s and '70s. I wasn't even sure my client was old enough to know who Sonny and Cher were, but Joanne showed me they were singing one of their greatest hits, "I Got You Babe." My client gasped again and began to weep. She told me that "I Got You Babe" was the song that Joanne and her husband used to sing to one another. It was something he would know to immediately recognize as unique to their relationship. My client consented to pass along Joanne's message to her widowed husband, and I only hope it offered him some comfort in his grief.

Of course, as was previously discussed, a common manner of after-life communication from a deceased loved one, especially a partner or spouse, is the visitation while in a dream state. Many a widow has felt such desperation for wanting to experience this spiritual gift that a blockage is created that can only be relieved by the passage of time and the lessening of the intense grief that is experienced following such a profound loss. I have had any number of women suffering such a loss question if they are being punished or if their deceased loved one doesn't still love them because they haven't enjoyed this special nighttime reunion during their sleep. Gently, I explain that no one is entitled to receive a visitation, that there are factors that may compromise or preclude a visitation (such as urgency, desperation and consuming grief), and that focusing on a visitation exclusively may prevent them from being attentive to other forms of communication from Spirit such as seemingly coincidental signs that prompt fond and loving memories of the one who has passed on. When the mind is relaxed and otherwise preoccupied is when the propensity is greatest for receiving these loving memorial tokens, which makes it that much sweeter for being completely unexpected.

After losing the love of your life, it may be inconceivable to consider a new romance; the chances of finding a love comparable to the love you lost may seem bleak and daunting, or even disrespectful to the loved one's memory. But believe it or not, on a number of occasions during psychic readings, I have been shown that is precisely what the deceased loved one desires most for the mate that has been left behind. More often than not, a former husband, boyfriend or even an ex-husband will come through in Spirit to convey that their love endures beyond the physical world, but they don't wish for my client to punish herself or feel guilty by denying herself the opportunity for a new happiness. They are clear in communicating that it doesn't alter or diminish what the client and they had together, because that was a separate and distinct relationship that cannot be duplicated.

Nor do loved ones in Spirit expect you to necessarily dive right into a new love affair, as that can have a rebound effect, which could prove to be an inauthentic motive for wanting a relationship—to regain, rekindle or forget the lost love. What Spirit has shown me, however, is the desire for my clients to have male companionship. This does not equate to a torrid love affair (which is how I think some of my clients interpret it). Instead, the male in Spirit will suggest it would be good to have a friend to go out to dinner with, take in a movie or a show, or travel with, without the expectation of anything else. They show me a new gentleman holding open the door for their lady or pulling out her chair in a restaurant; in essence, treating her as she deserves to be treated. Nothing is expected and nothing is imposed, just companionship.

In short, they want you to have romantic relationships and even remarry, if that is your prerogative. Curiously enough, where the latter is concerned, they sometimes pick the new partner! It is not uncommon after losing a partner or spouse, for longtime clients to return to tell me they are seriously dating or have otherwise paired up with someone unexpectedly. Sometimes their new man is the best friend or even the brother of the deceased, or somehow coincidentally (or not!) the deceased and the new man went to school together, worked together or otherwise crossed paths with one another years before.

Clients have told me of the odd or unusual ways in which the new connections have occurred, such as visiting a favorite point of destination in the former relationship and striking up a conversation with a stranger who turns out to be not as much of a stranger as initially thought. The deceased loved ones have shown me how they had a hand in orchestrating the timetable for each person's schedule to create the encounter opportunity. However, they do remind me of their "hands off" policy and that, while they pulled strings to make the meeting happen, it is not their place to interfere with anyone's free will if the chemistry simply isn't there. Still, it may provide some comfort to know that a deceased loved one is actually hoping you will not deny opportunities for a newfound love and are cheering you on to the point of having a hand in staging it.

Another source of guilt for those clients of mine who have been widowed is that of hanging on to the deceased loved one's personal possessions. I'll never forget facilitating a psychic event and connecting to the deceased husband of a woman in the audience. He identified himself by showing me that he played guitar and had an extensive record and CD collection for being so passionate about music. The woman responded that she was lamenting over what to do with all her husband's personal effects, including his music collection which was taking up space and collecting dust. Almost impulsively, I blurted out his response: "Honey, I don't give a fuck what you do with my shit." Red with embarrassment, I implored her to confirm that the reply sounded like something he would say, and, through her laughter and tears, she affirmed that was exactly something he would have said. (Boy, was I relieved!)

Her husband's point has been echoed by countless other loved ones in Spirit over the years, including not just deceased husbands and boyfriends but children, siblings and parents. And the point is this: In the Heavenly Realm, all ties to material possessions have been released. Usually, this extends beyond clothing and other personal effects to include boats, automobiles, homes, land and other real estate. Where the loved ones in Spirit presently exist, they can conjure whatever they wish merely by recalling it in memory. They have shown me fishing in a boat on the water or the cabin or hunting lodge in the woods that was a favorite vacation destination. In essence, and contrary to popular belief, you do get to take it with you, so long as it is emotionally relevant to you personally or to those who are left behind in the physical world. So, you can see why the matter of what to do with someone's belongings is rather moot; the ability to relive and reexperience it all is limited only by the memory and imagination of those in Spirit.

What Spirit has communicated, however, is a compassionate understanding of the struggle for those in mourning and the desire to maintain a degree of connectedness through the retention of certain physical objects. They acknowledge that the grieving process is precisely that, a process; and that it takes time to slowly purge and release someone's belongings, not because of the things themselves but because of the memories they harbor still. Oftentimes, there is a sense of guilt on the part of the surviving spouse for not wishing to insult or offend their loved one in Spirit by disposing of their property (thus the very blunt directive from the woman's husband during the preceding psychic event). This can be a very real struggle that may spawn agonizing anxiety and remorse for wanting to "do right" by the person who has passed on. Again, the response is not intended to minimize the relationship, but to emphasize that most personal possessions are of minimal significance in the grand scheme of the bigger picture.

The compromise comes when the loved one in Spirit suggests that their wife or girlfriend retain only those items that have sentimental value. Usually this is a ring or other piece of jewelry such as a watch or a chain. This recommendation makes sense when you consider that the metal, used to craft such objects, will retain the energy of the person who originally wore it or used it, as was noted before. This may not only offer direct comfort to those mourning a loss, it provides a vehicle by which Spirit may more readily connect to those left behind. This is because the metal object, and the emotion of the memory while holding it, combines to synchronize the connection between the soul frequencies, bridging the gap between the living and deceased. As was previously explained, this process actually has a name, it's called psychometry. Psychometry is precisely that: creating a connection to Spirit by gleaning intuitive impressions and sensations from holding an object that had belonged to someone else. (You can even practice doing this with a friend by swapping items belonging to others and see how accurate you are to describing individuals' attributes.) This also creates a psychic entrainment (remember that word?) between the Earthly, physical realm and the Spirit World.

In other instances, I've had deceased loved ones direct my attention to items they've collected or retained, the true value of which is unknown by their surviving kin. For example, a coin or stamp collection, or old stock certificates stored for safekeeping between the pages of old books or even tucked into a family Bible. Sometimes it is suggested that these things of monetary value should be consigned to auction, donated to those who want it (such as other collectors or a charitable organization or local historical society) or bequeathed to extended family as heirlooms. Where a client continues to waver, I've had their loved one in Spirit become more prescriptive by stating, "Okay, you can keep five things and get rid of the rest." This sort of direction may seem insensitive but it's really just the panacea necessary for the client to push forward in cleaning out clothes closets and drawers, or clearing out a basement, garage or attic workspace. And to the contrary, the message has always remained consistently the same: "Stop worrying about when your number's up, remember me fondly but keep moving forward, and enjoy the rest of your life with the time you have remaining. We will be reunited soon enough."

– Chapter 14 –

THE RICHES OF CONTENTMENT

Rarely do matters of the heart happen spontaneously and with any immediacy; a true romance with the promise of longevity should unfold naturally and organically. That's not to suggest that love at first sight cannot occur but it is an uncommon rarity anymore. This may be frustrating if you are not, by nature, a patient person and if you believe you've already tried everything to connect with an eligible man but have had no luck. In my work as a psychic, I meet many women who fit this description as you might imagine. Most of them have something in common, however. They are all fiercely independent, strongly opinionated and self-confident.

If a woman is a survivor of previous bad romances or even abusive relationships, they're not in a position to waste anybody's time; they know what they want and, more importantly, experience has taught them what they don't want. They have long ago arrived at the conclusion that they don't need a man to make them whole or complete. Oftentimes they are successful in their field of vocation or are prosperous entrepreneurs who have established a business reputation through blood, sweat and tears, and through sheer will of determination. Because of this grit (or as their father figures-in-Spirit call it, "moxie") they can hold their own against the fellas in male-dominated fields, such as real estate, marketing or business sales. This is not true in every case, but it is true in the case of those women who have understood that the secret meaning of life is to assess their past history—good, bad and indifferent—and finesse it to their advantage and employ it to their benefit (instead of surrendering to it).

Also true of such women is that they present themselves outwardly with a strength of resilience, a levity of spiritedness. They take good care of themselves and have learned how to accentuate their good points and physical assets. Thus, when I encounter them, they have a great smile, a firm handshake and are very attractive. Their makeup, hair, nails and clothing are usually impeccable and quite tasteful. Most importantly, they're not doing this for any one man; they're doing it as part and parcel of their business savvy so that they make a great first impression with their clientele. On the surface, then, these are gals that appear to have everything working in their favor. So why are they coming to me asking about when they'll find a man? It's a realization some of them haven't yet arrived at understanding.

The simple fact is that many men can't deal with strong, confident, attractive women. They are intimidated and perplexed by gals who don't need a man for financial support or are self-sufficient enough to live alone and still feel productive and whole. If you are in a particularly conservative or rural area, you may have noticed this for yourself. Traditional values and roles for women that are outdated for not being progressive enough are, indeed, oftentimes upheld. You surely don't want to be a man's maid, cook, laundress, housekeeper and sex object, especially if you've already been there, done that. And yet this is precisely what a lot of very conservative-thinking males expect of a female mate, believe it or not, still in this day and age.

I always recommend that gals who are strong, confident and attractive not change anything at all about themselves in order to appease obsolete male norms. They've worked too hard to earn what they've achieved to pretend to be anything less. Instead, I highlight their amazing growth and the extraordinary efforts invested into their personal development—something they may have lost sight of in its totality over time. I advise them not to lower their standards but to remain patient as there are available men who are self-assured enough to feel comfortable with a woman who has been successful; it may even be romantically or sexually stimulating to them.

These men tend to also be prosperous themselves, being impeccably educated, well-traveled, self-made executives, entrepreneurs or top-tier professionals. Oftentimes, they enjoy the fire of a sparring partner with whom they can debate with good-natured jabs and arguments in crackling give-and-take dialogue. They do exist; you just may need to cast a wider net in order to locate them in their natural environments. This could mean actively involving yourself in distinguished social, cultural, civic, charitable, recreational and sports activities— community environments that tend to attract your equals in the opposite sex: smart, successful gentlemen who are unfettered by intimidation because of a woman's own success and intelligence.

Women who outwardly present in ways that are strong, confident and attractive are also intimidating to men for another reason that often goes undiscussed: sexual performance anxiety. This has become a huge issue in recent years, and affects men of all ages but, increasingly so, men in their twenties and thirties. This is due to the proliferation and accessibility of pornography in which sex acts are choreographed and edited to appear free from faults, frailties and foibles. Instead, what is depicted has presented a warped and unrealistic expectation of what men should be capable of performing in the bedroom. I have seen this in my psychic work; some very young men have confessed to me that their anxiety over being intimate with a woman they perceive to be physically stunning has had a direct correlation to erectile dysfunction. Their fears of being sexually rejected, they think, risk becoming reality should they not achieve and maintain an erection. And they feel emasculated for having failed.

Pornography has also created another overarching issue for men that threatens to totally derail a sexual relationship with confident, successful women; and that is the size of their penis. Men who perform in pornographic videos are usually employed due to their stamina, libido and, yes, the thickness and length of their erect penis. It's not only a selling point, it gives the false impression that a man whose sexual prowess is fueled by his large penis is what every woman wants. Of course, this is not remotely true.

The average male already thinks he has a small penis because a) he's looking down on it, which skews perspective, making it look smaller than it really is, b) they don't have as many male communal opportunities anymore (such as locker rooms, group showers and urinals without dividers between them) to compare themselves against other typical males, and c) they are comparing themselves against the above-average penises that are abundant in pornography.

Most women could care less about whether or not a man is a sexual acrobat; they just want a good man with a good heart who will be good to them (and good to their children). What men don't realize, and what it is incumbent upon women to communicate, is that size doesn't matter, especially if a couple is in love. More than one female client of mine has invoked the old adage about disregarding the size of the boat in favor of the motion of the ocean, and most women are very understanding and forgiving. One client explained the humiliation her husband endures for having to inject his penis with a chemical stimulant in advance of having sex in order to attain a viable erection. She is very compassionate and patient because she loves her man.

Perhaps the most concerning aspect of modern pornography is that it has nearly legitimized slapping, choking and spitting—acts of degradation—as part and parcel of routine sex acts, giving the impression that a woman expects it! An entire generation of young men is growing up with the distorted thinking that this is normal bedroom behavior based on what they see, and how women and men in pornography behave. This is destructive and can only lead to a myriad of complications and serious issues, especially where such behavior is not consensual. The margin of division between romantic love and sex has broadened dramatically in recent times, and it will be for young women of the future to school their prospective mates on what is and is not acceptable conduct. Not all men watch pornography, of course, however, the man you partner with is a sexual being and most men have a sex drive that you do not control. In short, you have to let him look.

What this means is that you cannot keep your man on such a tight leash that he feels unable to privately exercise the sexual aspect of his personhood. He's obviously attracted to you, otherwise he wouldn't be in a committed relationship. But he finds other women attractive too, same as you can admire a handsome man. He may masturbate while fantasizing about famous female celebrities, or he may stare longing or even lustfully at good-looking women online or in person. Rather than create unnecessary drama by blowing up (and out of proportion) such incidents, one of my clients took a laid-back approach. She shared that when she and her boyfriend went out to dinner, she caught him eyeing the pretty waitress, who was their server, as she walked away to place their order. Instead of telegraphing any insecurity, she countered his ogling by saying, "She's got a great figure, doesn't she?" Her boyfriend turned red faced and responded with, "Okay, you caught me. I'm busted!" They both had a good chuckle and the situation was diffused. This was a savvy, intelligent way of acknowledging her boyfriend's sex drive while also acknowledging that she noticed his noticing behavior, thus putting him on notice!

As was said earlier, a common theme revealed through my mediumship, by mothers and fathers in Spirit who did not have successful marriages, is that of the wife withholding sex from the husband as a punishment. This is never an effective strategy, but a tactic employed by women to gain (or regain) some control but which, to their spouse, feels entirely manipulative. It almost poses an impossible challenge: Is this scheme supposed to cajole the husband into finding the wife more desirable for having to practically plead? Or does it set the stage for the inevitable affair by the husband who can longer meet the expectation of both monogamy and celibacy? If you are someone who grew up in a household in which this power dynamic occurred, please give consideration to the motives of both parties under such circumstances. Oftentimes, the formerly needy mother, now that she is deceased, will confess with the clarity of hindsight that withholding sex was symptomatic of severe depression, among many other issues. They used this scheme as part of the victim routine, facilitating with ease the accusing and blaming of others for their misery. And the accusations and blame usually portrayed the husband and father as the prime villain. More than one deceased mother in Spirit has been emphatic in revealing that she biased her children against their father, admitting her wrongdoing. It is important, then, not to replicate this behavior as it is not at all effective.

You may therefore appreciate that so much of successful compatibility is unlearning your past while simultaneously learning from his. Is he competitive, a workaholic, a martyr, or the golden boy? If so, it may be traced to his upbringing and the influences of his family circumstances. You'll be able to validate this clearly once you meet his surviving siblings if his parents are not also still living. These relationships will also provide valuable insights and clues—or perhaps even red flags—to indicate the struggles that await you if you decide to advance the relationship. Thus, the length of a compatible relationship is due an ever-shifting flexibility for adapting and accommodating one another depending upon one another's moods and feelings. And remember: The absence of communication is a form of communication.

Speaking of the absence of communication, it seems as though any number of gals believe that they are indeed communicating that they love and adore their man; but then wonder why he doesn't seem to recognize or acknowledge all that they do which, from their perspective, conveys this without question. The problem is, they are communicating this through their actions and not their words. Recall that your fella may not be the most intuitive of souls (until you test out the psychic exercises described previously in this book). This means that he is unlikely to pick up on all the subtleties that are so obvious to you but that go largely unnoticed by him.

For example, you might think that picking up his favorite dessert on your way home or texting him words of encouragement during the day clearly communicates how you feel about him; but he might simply equate these niceties as thoughtful instead of underscoring how much you love him. Don't discontinue doing these things but also be direct and to the point by stating, "I love you!" Conversely, remember to stroke him with compliments instead of, again, assuming that he is clueing in on your appreciation. In short, say what you mean and mean what you say, and there'll be little margin for error and misinterpretation. (And, attendant to the previous discussion on male sexual hangups, telling him that he's a great lover never hurts!)

Until you find a male companion, consider how much of your time you invest in being anxious or worried about being partnerless. Is it a consuming void or are you able to balance the desire with priorities such as career, hobbies and interest, or your children and pets. Do you like yourself? Given your family history and past relationships, loving yourself may be tough; but if you can at least feel comfortable with who you are, then maybe you'd be willing to date yourself if you were a man. When you stop the counterproductive wondering and worrying and focus on being a decent human being who knows who she is and is passionate for the things she finds important or inspiring, the culmination of the output you radiate will be reciprocated. It's called karma; you get back what you put out.

It's the same as when people are grieving the loss of a loved one and expect and demand a message from Spirit. When nothing is forthcoming, they may feel unloved or punished. But when they relax and focus on living their lives, the message tends to manifest when they least expect it. Know that resiliency is not an absence of adversity but the ability to persevere in the face of it. When it comes to affairs of the heart, above all else, the single most important thing you can do is learn to trust your own intuition. Ultimately, it will serve you well.

ABOUT THE AUTHOR

William Stillman is the internationally known, award-winning author of ten special needs parenting books including Autism and the God *Connection*, *The Soul of Autism*, and *The Autism Prophecies*, a trilogy that correlates aspects of autism with metaphysical themes. Stillman's work has resonated with parents, professionals, and persons with autism internationally, and has received endorsements of praise from bestselling authors and spiritual pioneers Gary Zukav, Carol Bowman, Dean Hamer, and Larry Dossey. To date, his books have been translated in four languages.

Stillman's spiritual work led to him contributing a week of daily reflections for the 2009 edition of *Disciplines: A Book of Daily Devotions,* and creating a training module for The Thoughtful Christian, a Web-based resource organization. His book *Conversations with Dogs: A Psychic Reveals What Our Canine Companions Have to Say (And How You Can Talk to Them Too!)* was published in 2015 and a new edition was printed in 2018 by Haunted Road Media. *Under Spiritual Siege: How Ghosts and Demons Affect Us and How to Combat Them*, about spiritual warfare with negative energies, was published in 2016, and his book, *The Secret Language of Spirit: Understanding Spirit Communication in Our Everyday Lives*, was released in 2017. In 2018, *The Secret Language of Spirit* was named a finalist in the National Indie Excellence Book Awards. Most recently, *The Practicing Psychic: An Essential Guide for Staying Grounded, Navigating Skeptics and Honoring Your Gift* was published in by Haunted Road Media 2021.

Additionally, since 1989, Stillman has coauthored six bestselling and critically-acclaimed books on *The Wizard of Oz*, most recently *The Road to Oz: The Evolution, Creation, and Legacy of a Motion Picture Masterpiece*, which won the 2019 National Indie Excellence Book Award in its respective category.

Stillman has worked professionally as a psychic medium and spiritual counselor since 2004. His accuracy in discerning the truth and making predictions that come to fruition has been acclaimed by his clients as truly extraordinary. He is regularly consulted on missing person and unsolved homicide cases. He also volunteers his time as an investigative resource to the Pennsylvania Paranormal Association. In 2024, Stillman was vetted and certified for the Bob Olson's Best Psychic Directory online.

Stillman has been interviewed on numerous radio shows of a paranormal nature including Coast to Coast AM, the most listened to overnight radio program in North America. He has twice been interviewed on the Web series CharVision by internationally renowned psychic medium Char Margolis, who called Stillman "really fascinating," and he has been a guest on the popular YouTube series Swedenborg and Life. Stillman has been a repeated guest speaker for Lily Dale Assembly near Jamestown, NY, the country's oldest and most revered spiritualist community.

Stillman's web site is www.williamstillman.com and his Facebook page is William Stillman Psychic Medium.

Other William Stillman titles from Haunted Road Media:

THE PRACTICING PSYCHIC

The Practicing Psychic is the culmination of award-winning author William Stillman's perspective and insight gleaned from his more than 17 years of professional work as a psychic medium and spiritual advisor. With accessible language, easy-to-understand explanations, and compelling anecdotes, Stillman walks the budding psychic practitioner through the ins and outs of the business aspects of the field, as well as navigating clients, skeptics, and unusual situations such as encountering ghosts.

CONVERSATIONS WITH DOGS

Have you ever wanted to know what your dog would say if he could talk? Now you can! Believe it or not, our canine companions have a lot to say beyond eat, drink, sniff, play and protect. In this fascinating new book, psychic William Stillman explores the dialogues he's had with dogs and reveals their inner most thoughts about their owners, their roles and the cycle of life.